FHSW

SWNHS

WS
S18
SHA

C20094422

Library
Knowledge Spa
Royal Cornwall Hospital
Treliske
Truro. TR1 3HD

D0302803

YOUNG DISABLED PEOPLE

Monitoring Change in Education

Series Editor:
Cedric Cullingford
University of Huddersfield, UK

Change is a key characteristic of the worlds of business, education and industry and the rapidity of change underlines an urgent need to analyze, evaluate and, where appropriate, correct its direction. The series is aimed at contributing to this analysis. Its unique contribution consists of making sense of changes in education and in offering a timely and considered response to new challenges; the series, therefore, focuses on contemporary issues and does so with academic rigour.

Other titles in the series

Literacy and Schooling
Towards Renewal in Primary Education Policy
Kathy Hall
ISBN 978 0 7546 4179 7

Globalisation, Education and Culture Shock
Edited by
Cedric Cullingford and Stan Gunn
ISBN 978 0 7546 4201 5

Risk, Education and Culture
Edited by
Andrew Hope and Paul Oliver
ISBN 978 0 7546 4172 8

Race and Ethnicity in Education
Ranjit Arora
ISBN 978 0 7546 1441 8

Mentoring in Education
An International Perspective
Edited by
Cedric Cullingford
ISBN 978 0 7546 4577 1

Young Disabled People
Aspirations, Choices and Constraints

SONALI SHAH
University of Leeds, UK

ASHGATE

© Sonali Shah 2008

All rights reserved. No part of this publication may be reproduced, stored in a retrieval system or transmitted in any form or by any means, electronic, mechanical, photocopying, recording or otherwise without the prior permission of the publisher.

Sonali Shah has asserted her right under the Copyright, Designs and Patents Act, 1988, to be identified as the author of this work.

Published by
Ashgate Publishing Limited
Wey Court East
Union Road
Farnham
Surrey GU9 7PT
England

Ashgate Publishing Company
Suite 420
101 Cherry Street
Burlington, VT 05401-4405
USA

www.ashgate.com

British Library Cataloguing in Publication Data
Shah, Sonali, 1973-
  Young disabled people : aspirations, choices and
  constraints. - (Monitoring change in education)
  1. Young adults with disabilities - Employment - Great
  Britain 2. Youth with disabilities - Education - Great
  Britain 3. Vocational rehabilitation - Great Britain
  I. Title
  362.4'0484'0842

Library of Congress Cataloging-in-Publication Data
Shah, Sonali, 1973-
  Young disabled people : aspirations, choices and constraints / by Sonali Shah.
      p. cm. -- (Monitoring change in education)
  Includes bibliographical references and index.
  ISBN 978-0-7546-7422-1
  1. Young adults with disabilities--Employment--Great Britain. 2. Youth with disabilities-
  -Employment--Great Britain. 3. Young adults with disabilities--Education--Great Britain.
  4. Vocational rehabilitation--Great Britain. I. Title.

  HD7256.G7S53 2008
  331.3'40870941--dc22

                                                                    2008031812

ISBN 978 0 7546 7422 1

Mixed Sources
Product group from well-managed
forests and other controlled sources
www.fsc.org Cert no. SGS-COC-2482
© 1996 Forest Stewardship Council
FSC

Printed and bound in Great Britain by
TJ International Ltd, Padstow, Cornwall

Contents

Acknowledgements   *vii*

1   Introduction, Background and Policy   1

2   Career Development and Choices of Young People   15

3   Young People's Aspirations: What Are They and Why?   31

4   Choices and Opportunities in Mainstream and Special Education   49

5   How Families Shape the Choices of Young Disabled People   77

6   Conclusion: Discussion and Young People's Ideas for Change   93

Bibliography   *103*
Index   *121*

Acknowledgements

This book could not have been written without the support and generosity of many people out there.

I would like to thank the European Social Fund for funding the postdoctoral research on which this book is based.

This research would not have been possible without all of the young disabled people and educational professionals who took part in it. Many thanks for letting me into your schools and so generously taking the time to share your stories and dreams with me. The young disabled people will appear under pseudonyms in this text.

Special thanks are due to my two supervisors, Professor Robert Walker and Professor Gillian Pascall, who have given me constant support and encouragement throughout the course of the three-year project on which this book is based. Their constructive comments on the development of the research and this text have played a critical role in the progression of my own learning and the creation of this book. Thanks to Professor Cedric Cullingford who believed the research was worthwhile.

Many thanks to the project advisory group: Dean Thomas, Ian Beadle, Gordon Jamieson, Amanda Payne and Chris Harrison. Also, an important and indeed memorable part of the research would not have been possible without the support and professional expertise of my friend and drama colleague Nicky Wildin, and my two research support assistants Nicola Kilvington and Melissa Walker. I am very grateful to my friend Dr Sarah Woodin for spending her time and energy proofreading the manuscript and offering excellent advice. Finally I would like to thank Anna Williams for her formatting skills.

Chapter 1
Introduction, Background and Policy

Work and Society

In all industrialized countries, paid employment is central to the economy of the state and to the status, health and prosperity of the individual. Having a job is one of the most significant issues in any adult's life and preparing young people for work in subsequent years is often the primary aim of schools. From an early age young people are taught that employment is one of the principal indicators of successful adulthood and social inclusion. They are encouraged to equip themselves with the skills and qualifications necessary to secure good employment in their subsequent lives. They learn, either implicitly or directly, about the consequences of unemployment including the threat of poverty, social exclusion and a lack of political or social status in society.

An individual's status in economic society is somewhat determined by the expectations and ideologies of many agents of socialization and the psychosocial structure of society (that is, the social factors and individual interactive behaviour that influence the composition of society). Knowledge of an individual's status indicates their social and political beliefs and their resultant placement in the social system. Furthermore it reflects some of their characteristics, patterns of behaviour, and expectations others have of them. As Vroom (1964) argues, a person's status greatly influences the way in which other people respond to them. For instance, according to Young (1981), doctors are often viewed as God-like figures – strong, powerful, clever and in control of some kind of magic. This popular, socially approved image of health professionals can, itself, be a barrier for disabled people, who are generally perceived as being too weak and ineffective (French 1986) to succeed as health and caring professionals. It is possible that some of these negative perceptions of disabled people may colour professional attitudes, albeit unconsciously, and thus cause aspirations to follow an otherwise conventional career path to be rejected.

Numerous studies suggest that, like women and people from ethnic minorities, young disabled people are strongly influenced by others' perceptions of their achievements. Schools and families, the two social structures discussed in Chapters 4 and 5 of this book, have a significant part to play in shaping the choices and aspirations of young disabled people. This is not only in terms of what subjects they learn within the formal school curriculum, but also interaction with teachers and parents, exposure to information about types of work and professional roles, level of inclusion in mainstream society and the number of encounters with disabling barriers. Furthermore what is expected of young disabled people, by various social structures in their lives, does somewhat determine what choices they can make and the extent to which their original aspirations become reality. For instance, if disabled people are not expected to become doctors or nurses, they are unlikely to be taught the relevant subjects at school, or see disabled doctors on the media, or be able to access necessary qualifications and buildings where work experience is located.

Exclusion from the paid labour market is clearly evident. Burchardt (2005) found that the gap between the proportion of disabled and non-disabled people out of work widens as they get older. Around 60 per cent of disabled people of working age are not in paid work, with unemployment rates three times higher than for their non-disabled counterparts, while periods of unemployment have been much longer, particularly for people born with an impairment (Burchardt 2000). One in six of those who acquire an impairment while in paid work lose their job within a year, and a third of disabled people who find paid work become unemployed again within a year, compared with one-fifth of non-disabled people (Burchardt 2000). Disabled people earn significantly less, and approximately 50 per cent of disabled people have incomes below the 'official' poverty line of less than half the national average wage, with disabled women particularly disadvantaged (Burchardt 2000; Martin, White and Meltzer 1989). Moreover, a significant proportion of disabled people between 55 and 64 years of age have been moved into early retirement. Disabled people also experience higher levels of underemployment in jobs for which they are 'overqualified' (Walker 1982). An analysis of labour market trends in 2001 by Smith and Twomey (2002) indicated that there are fewer than average disabled people employed in Social Class I of the Registrar Generals Classification of Occupations, including managers, senior officials, professionals and associate professionals. Smith and Twomey (2002) report that a high proportion of disabled people are concentrated in semi-skilled and skilled labour such as administrative and secretarial roles, skilled trades, personal services and elementary occupations.

Over the past decade the UK government has implemented a number of strategies for supporting the transition of young people and disabled people into work. The aim has been to ensure that all those who can, will compete for paid employment in the free market (Grover and Piggott 2005). The New Deal for Disabled People was accepted by local authorities as the mechanism for achieving employment targets for disabled people, and Jobcentre Plus and their contracted job broker organizations are formally required to address the needs of disabled people who are unemployed. The New Deal for Disabled People and the Personal Advisor Service, launched in 1998, aimed to provide individually tailored packages of support to help people in work and at risk of losing their jobs through ill health or impairment to move towards and stay in work. The 1995 Disability Discrimination Act (DDA), and its extension in 2005, gives disabled people certain rights in the UK with respect to employment. In particular the DDA makes it unlawful for an employer to discriminate against disabled people when they apply for a job, or when they are in employment, unless they can show that making necessary adjustments would be unreasonable. In this way the law also defines when discrimination is legitimate. This statute is meant to protect disabled people from discrimination on the grounds of their impairment, and is part of a new focus on helping unemployed disabled people into work whether they are claiming benefits or not. The Disability Task Force, established by New Labour in 1997 to assess the 1995 Act, set up the Disability Rights Commission in 1999 to orchestrate future disability discrimination policy.

Other recent government initiatives, such as the Department of Work and Pension's (DWP) Access to Work and Pathways to Work schemes, offer a package of support to help disabled people return to the workforce or to retain people who become disabled while in employment. Employers can use Access to Work to eliminate the potential costs of employing disabled people, costs that would put them at a disadvantage when competing for employment with non-disabled counterparts (Grover and Piggott 2005).

Young People and Society

The economic future of society critically depends on the success of the young people of today. Recognizing this, the government has launched new strategies to support the transition of young people into work. The New Deal for Young People, introduced in January 2005 in selected areas and extended to the whole of the UK in April, is a major welfare-to-work programme in the UK targeted at 18–24-year-old unemployed people on job seekers allowance. The aim of the programme is to enhance employability at both the extensive (finding a job) and intensive (long-term employment) margins, while acquiring skills and motivation.

However, the support systems and barriers for young disabled people outlined in the government's policy agenda may well differ from young disabled people's perceptions about what facilitates and restricts their educational development and transition to meet occupational aspirations. Disabled people's experience of early adult life continues to be beset with frustration and disappointment; their original aspirations are rarely translated into concrete occupational or educational achievements (Burchardt 2005). As Professor Al Aynsley-Green, the Children's Commissioner, states:

When I listen to young people with disability they are very concerned about the future, that they will drop off the cliff into a black hole of what they see to be people who do not understand the issue. (Evidence taken before the Department of Education and Skills, House of Commons, December 2005, available from <http://www.parliament. the-stationary-office.co.uk/pa/cm200506/cmselect/cmeduski/723/5120502.htm>)

If young disabled people's needs are to be met, disabled people need to be able to participate in processes and not just consulted in the development of new services.

There is much evidence that disabled teenagers seem to express hopes and fears about their 'future selves' that are shaped less by their impairment status than by other social influences (Norwich 1997). In particular, disabled children's aspirations about future employment and family life seem to reflect those of non-disabled children (Burchardt 2005; Morris 2002). However, they require specific action to tackle the disabling barriers they experience. Services that seek to support young disabled people in their transition to adulthood can make all the difference to what happens to them. If young disabled people have information about these services, and support to achieve their aspired goals and to combat the disabling barriers created by societal structures, there is less chance that they will experience an adult life of dependency and low expectations (Morris 2002).

Listening to Children

The views of disabled school children are often ignored. Often they are not consulted about major questions that affect them (Beecher 1998; Beresford 1997; Russell 1998). Furthermore they have less freedom to make choices about their social and personal life.

A body of research has argued that disabled children and young people are consigned to a passive role rather than being seen as active subjects who should be fully included in those processes which have a bearing on their lives (Priestley 1998). This has often had the effect of objectifying and silencing disabled children. As a consequence, research has often concealed the roles of disabled children as social actors, negotiating complex identities and social relationships within a disabling environment, and as agents of change who can adapt to, challenge and inform the individuals, cultures and institutions that they encounter during their childhoods.

There is a growing recognition that gaining the views of young people is crucial for understanding issues that affect their lives. Professor Aynsley-Green suggests this involves policy-makers listening to children and young people and ensuring that every policy and legislation is embedded in what they say.

However, to date, very little is known about the way in which children, especially disabled children, make sense of their identities, and create a sense of their past and their imagined futures over time (Neale and Flowerdew 2004). Although there is growing recognition of children's competence in being involved in decisions about their health, welfare and education, most social policy initiatives are still designed, delivered and evaluated by adults, be they teachers, parents or politicians. Adult conceptions of childhood are at best partial, with limited connection to the views and experiences of children and young people in twenty-first-century Britain (Prout 2001; Such, Walker and Walker 2005). Children are referred to as weak, passive and impressionable, and rarely presented as powerful, strong and competent (Such, Walker and Walker 2005).

A body of work (see, for instance Priestley 1998; Shakespeare and Watson 1998) suggests that, historically, disabled children have been characterized by narratives of dependence, vulnerability and exclusion, and described as a homogeneous group with few rights and choices to enable them to achieve universal standardized targets (Morris 1997). However, to accept such a theory would be to ignore social differences around gender, social class, minority group status, sexuality and age, and therefore refuse to acknowledge all children as individual social actors, regardless of their physicality. Young people are active social agents, able to communicate their own experiences and express their own views (O'Kane 2000). Therefore children and young people should be key informants for professionals, regarding issues that routinely become important at particular points in their life course.

Aim of the Book

Recent policies and government initiatives across education, health and social services have strengthened expectations that professionals will involve disabled young people in decisions that affect their futures. The Code of Practice on the Identification and Assessment of Special Educational Needs (DFEE 2001) states that children have the right to be heard and should be encouraged to participate in any decision-making process to meet their special educational needs (Read and Clements 2001). Further, legislation such as the Disability Discrimination Act (1995; 2005), the Human Rights Act (1998) and the Special Educational Needs and Disability Act (2001) have provided disabled people with the right to participate and compete with their non-disabled peers in mainstream education and employment. Despite these initiatives, however, there still remains a large gap between the voices of disabled children/young people and the imposition of policy. Cullingford (2002) argues that although many maintain that children should have the right to be heard, few put this into practice.

Research into the perspectives of young disabled people has been limited. Education decisions and career-related choices, as well as young disabled people's perceptions of how these have been shaped, have not been given due weight. Furthermore, when the primary focus of research has been about career choices and aspirations, it has been in connection with non-disabled young people (see, for instance, Foskett and Hemsley-Brown 2001; Hodkinson and Sparkes 1997; Kidd 1984).

This book is particularly timely because it gives disabled students a voice to inform current policy about issues that affect their lives. It affords young disabled people an opportunity to voice their aspirations in terms of why and where they originated, how they could be achieved, and the structures that might influence how their aspirations can be met. This book presents evidence to suggest that young people's choices may be enabled or obstructed by physical, social or attitudinal factors, either inherent to the individual (impairment, ethnicity, gender) or societal structures (friends, family, education, public services and the labour market).

The research basis for this book explores the practices, policies and social structures that determine the extent to which young disabled people achieve their planned aspirations or redirect their goals. It will reveal the similarities and differences that occur as a consequence of whether the young people attended special or mainstream education, and what age they are.

The findings will inform educationalists, employers and policy-makers in particular about what young disabled people want from their futures, and the structures necessary to facilitate their development.

The Young Disabled People

For the purposes of this book the term 'young disabled people' defines males and females, aged 13–25, who are in full-time education (in school or further education college) with physical impairments relating to mobility, dexterity and speech. The terms 'disabled people' and 'people with physical disabilities' are used interchangeably in this book, to mean: 'Individuals with mobility, dexterity and/ or speech impairments whose life development and choices have been influenced by their individual differences as well as social structures in society'. Thinking of disability in this way acknowledges the importance of the embodied experiences of disabled people as well as the part played by social processes and environments.

The central part of this book is taken from empirical research with 33 young people with physical impairments who were recruited from seven educational institutions within one city and one county within the East Midlands in the UK. These included two special schools (one with a sixth form unit), two mainstream secondary schools, two mainstream sixth form schools and one specialist further education college.

Table 1.1   The Young People

Name	Type of School/College	Age	Gender	Aspiration/s
Allan	Mainstream School (Age 11–18, Inaccessible 6th form)	13	Male	'Want to do something to do with computer games, or something fun I'll enjoy'
Joe	Mainstream School (Age 11–18)	13	Male	'I want to work with my dad fixing people's heaters … I wanted to be a PE teacher'
Millie	Mainstream School (Age 11–18)	13	Female	'I've got quite a few choices. I've got dance choreographer, and a singer or an actress'
Xavier	Mainstream School (Age 11–18)	13	Male	'I would like to look at games and computer games and review them … I'd like to sell stuff in a shop, a games shop'
Cathy	Special School	14	Female	'Too early, not sure … I would like to answer phones in an office'
Jenny	Mainstream School (Age 11–18, Inaccessible 6th form)	14	Female	'I want to go to a performing arts college to do acting and singing'
Nay	Mainstream School (Age 11–16)	14	Male	'I either want to work in sports industry or computer industry' 'I'd like to be a kind of DJ'
Pete	Mainstream School (Age 11–16)	14	Male	'I want to be a nursery school teacher … I want to teach children to read and write'
Sabrina	Mainstream School (Age 11–18)	14	Female	'I want to be a language interpreter, French and Spanish'
Sally	Mainstream School (Age 11–18)	14	Female	'I'll probably do something to do with computers' 'I wanted to do hairdressing but …'
Checka	Mainstream School (Age 11–16)	15	Female	'I want to be a superstar that shines very bright'
Dan	Mainstream School (Age 11–16)	15	Male	'I'd say I want to do either carpentry or joinery or both'
Ikky	Mainstream School (Age 11–16)	15	Male	'I want to do IT, like knowing the computer and putting programmes on them'

Mike	Mainstream School (Age 11–18)	15	Male	'I've always wanted to go into journalism, more than that I've always wanted to go over to writing books, but journalism's just like a back-up career'
Noalga	Special School	15	Male	'I want to do ICT maybe multimedia'
Quentin	Special School	15	Male	Don't know
Tim	Mainstream School (Age 11–18)	15	Male	'I'd like to be a coach driver … Or probably making music for someone' 'Live in my own house'
Tommo	Mainstream School (Age 11–16)	15	Male	'I want to do like a sports assistant'
Rob	Special School	16	Male	'I might I might be going for a job at Theatre Royal … Like doing a proper job, like doing the tickets on the door'
Sam	Mainstream School (Age 11–18)	17	Male	'I want to sort of go to university … I'll probably do something to do with either business or media … Possible jobs would probably be writing for TV or newspaper or something like that'
Steve	Mainstream School (Age 11–18)	17	Male	'It's always been my long-term aim to go to uni … I want to do an English Literature degree … and a job involving writing more than teaching … maybe a little bit of freelance writing'
Zoë	Special School (6th form)	17	Female	'I really want to live independently on my own … I want to go into employment, working with pregnant women right up to elderly people'
Fiona	Special School (6th form)	18	Female	'I wanted to do beauty first but …' 'Now I want to do photography after college. I haven't really thought about what sort of photography'
Hannah	Special School (6th form)	18	Female	'I'm hoping to do photography, and then maybe get a job in fashion photography'

Jane	Special College (residential)	18	Female	'I know I want to do something to do with drama, I want to be on *Coronation Street*'
Bob	Special School (6th form)	19	Male	'...learn independent skills to help mum with all the work ... I always wanted to be a DJ but I can't'
Maggie	Special School (until age 11) Pupil Referral Unit (Age 11–13) Mainstream School (Age 14–16)	19	Female	'When I was about 13, I was so horrified by the attitude of school that I wanted to be a journalist so I could expose it'
Tyson	Special School (6th form)	19	Female	'I want to do something connected with drama'
Paul	Special College (residential)	20	Male	'I want to do joinery at college, plus paint and decorate people's houses'
Schumacher	Special College (residential)	20	Female	'I'm looking towards a mainstream job in childcare'
Harry	Special College (residential)	21	Male	'I want to try and get a job where I live, with computers, doing web design'
Bella	Special College (residential)	22	Female	'After college I hope to get a job working with deaf people in the youth club'
Nick	Special College (residential)	23	Male	'I want to work with computers' 'I want to live independently'

The sample included men and women with different types of physical and sensory impairments including congenital, acquired and deteriorating conditions, and those who used a communication device in preference to speech. The school students were all aged between 13 and 19, and college students were aged between 16 and 25. Participants were from a variety of different social class, ethnic and cultural backgrounds. The young people were expected to participate in educational or vocational decision-making, focusing on significant transitional points of choice. These points coincided with the following four age bands: 13–15, 15–16, 16–18 and 19–25. This also corresponded to the points in time when the Connexions services are available to disabled people. The sample is illustrative rather than representative of the choices, aspirations and constraints of young disabled people.

Details of the young disabled people, including their name, type of school/college, their age, their gender and their aspirations for their futures (at the time the research was carried out) are summarized in Table 1.1 above. The young people chose alternative names for themselves to retain anonymity.

The Researcher and the Researched

I adopted a range of methods broadly subsumed within a qualitative methodology. Qualitative research enables access to groups such as disabled people and children, who are difficult to reach if quantitative techniques are used. The qualitative data generation methods used in this study included classroom observation, group discussions using forum theatre workshops and individual interviews. These tools were used to generate young disabled people's stories about their lives, allowing me to understand how they made particular decisions about their occupational futures.

It may be argued that the acquisition of rich quality data during this study, was facilitated by the fact that the interviewer and the participants came from the same minority group; that is, both parties shared experiences of challenging oppression, disablement, special education and partial integration. My ontological position, as a disabled researcher, was key to the development of this research. Leicester (1999) and Oakley (1981) suggest that interviewing individuals with similar experiences encourages the generation of richer material. Stanley and Wise (1993) describe this experience of knowing as an 'epistemological privilege' with researchers having access to a priori knowledge of their informants' subjective realities by virtue of their shared experiences.

This shared culture and background between the participants and myself was also helpful in accessing potential respondents, and building rapport with them, encouraging them to be more open. However, I was aware of the dangers of 'overrapport', and, taking Moser's (1958, 187–8) advice, adopted a 'pleasantness and a business-like nature'. Further, the fact I was disabled myself engendered positive role-modelling effects, encouraging the young disabled people to ask me questions about my own life, including whether I had encountered similar barriers to themselves when growing up and the coping strategies I used to overcome them. Several asked me about my life choices and trajectories, and the strategies I adopted to achieve my personal and professional choices in a society often perceived as working against disabled people. As I argue elsewhere (Shah 2006), although I was in danger of skewing the findings by my responses to the young people's questions, I was also conscious that the young people had given me their time, co-operation and confidences on some personal and difficult matters in their life, matters that they had every reason not to disclose to a stranger. For these reasons I owed them honest answers to their questions.

However, no research is completely free of bias. It is recognized that the closer our subject matter is to our own life, the more we can expect our own world view to enter into and shape our work and to influence the questions we pose and the interpretations we generate from our findings (Shah 2006). I argue that there is a thin dividing line between identification with one's research subjects and their exploitation (Reay 1996). Power-laden differences, whether race, gender or disablement, all have potential to disrupt any possibility of identification between the researcher and the researched. Finch (1984) has pointed out how, if interviewers assume commonalities and identification in the context of such differences, they are liable to reproduce structures of oppression and exploit research respondents. Thus reflexivity, the examination of how my own social reality influences the data collected and picture of the social world produced (Vernon 1997) is a critical exercise for those researching oppression.

As a British Indian professional disabled woman, in my mid-thirties, I was still able to retain a certain level of objectivity as a researcher because only part of my life history resembled that of each respondent. Bondi (2003) contends that this state enables the interviewer to be emotionally present and reactive to the interviewees' responses while simultaneously staying in touch with, and reflecting on, their own feelings. In this way there is not a danger of the interviewer becoming unconsciously overwhelmed by the respondents' stories, 'reacting to rather than reflecting on what is going on, and blurring the interviewer/interviewee boundary' (Shah 2006, 212).

Collecting What Young Disabled People Say

Research data was generated using three methods. Detailed analysis of the methods adopted and the reasons behind this has been written about elsewhere (see Shah 2006). For the purpose of this book a brief synopsis of the three phases of fieldwork is adequate. However, I will explain my motivations for using the methods to capture the views and experiences of young disabled people and also discuss the ethical issues surrounding confidentiality and anonymity.

Teachers or Special Educational Needs Co-ordinators (SENCOs) identified children who might participate in the research. Recruitment of students was, on the whole, based on the research sample criteria outlined in a research booklet which was sent to each school and college prior to the start of the fieldwork. The booklet stated the aims and objectives of the research and included a written consent form that was to be signed by the young people, or parents or guardians (in cases where young people were under the age of 18). The consent form emphasized that maintaining respect for the young people's views was crucial. Therefore, although what the young people said would be used in published material, their identities would be anonymized and remain confidential. However, as the purpose of this work is to listen to children's voices, care was taken not to erase their identities completely. As Morrow and Richards (1996a) point out, there are contradictions when researching children and young people because on the one hand children are regarded as vulnerable, incompetent and powerless, while also having the right to get their voice heard.

The first phase of the fieldwork involved classroom observation. This gave me, the researcher, an opportunity to observe how the young disabled people interacted with their peers and teachers in different contexts such as the classroom or the playground. There were two fundamental reasons for using observation as a research tool with young disabled people. The first was to collect bites of information about specific issues and concerns the young people had, which could be explored with them in the subsequent interviews. This not only guided the development of the interview schedule, but ensured that the questions reflected the young people's concerns and assumptions, not those of the researcher. The second reason for doing the observation was for me, the researcher, to become familiar with the school environment and also make myself known to potential participants.

The second phase of the fieldwork involved forum theatre workshops, with each group of young people in each of the seven educational institutions participating in the research. The objective of forum theatre workshops are discussed elsewhere (see Boal 2002; Fitzgerald, Jobling and Kirk, 2003; Shah 2006). For the purposes of the study, they were perceived as an exciting, non-threatening way to engage the young disabled people in debates about making choices, meeting aspirations and overcoming disabling barriers. Furthermore the workshops triggered thoughts about their own future selves including about employment, qualifications, support and barriers that would be explored in the third phase of the research, the personal interviews. The purpose of introducing the young people to the research and researcher prior to the interview phase was to encourage the young disabled people to talk lucidly about their experiences and aspirations without the awkwardness they might feel when being interviewed by a stranger.

This brings me on to the final phase of the fieldwork, the personal interviews with the young people. These were semi-structured, conducted within the young person's educational environment, and typically lasted between 20 and 40 minutes. With the permission of the young people and, where they were under age 18, their parents, the interviews were recorded and fully transcribed. Interviews covered the themes of family, school experiences, disabling barriers, relationships and future employment aspirations. Although each interview was guided by the same topic-setting questions, the young people chose to bring up important issues that were individual to their own circumstances.

The empirical research is integrated with existing theory and discussed in the following chapters:

Young People's Aspirations: What Are They and Why?

This is concerned with young disabled people's desired goals, including what they are, why and how they were chosen, and how the young disabled people think these goals could be achieved. The chapter will also examine the kinds of barriers to successful goal achievement that young disabled people experience and anticipate, and the consequences of failed trajectories. It explores how personal factors such as impairment, gender and age influence young disabled people's original aspirations and subsequent choices. The chapter discusses the extent to which the young people's choices are wide-ranging or specific, and reasons behind this.

Choices and Opportunities in Mainstream and Special Education

Education and the experience of schooling is an important determinant for vocational choice. This chapter is concerned with how young disabled people's formal and informal experiences in special and mainstream education shapes their choices and aspirations for their future lives. It explores the timely debate about educational segregation and inclusion of disabled children/young people, bringing in the perspectives of young disabled people who are currently based in mainstream and special education.

How Families Shape the Choices of Young Disabled People

The principal focus here is on the ways in which young disabled people perceive their family to influence their aspirations, especially in relation to future employment. There is a significant body of discourse to suggest that the family, a principal agent of primary socialization, is important for young people's career choices. This book examines how young disabled people consider their parents and siblings as influencing their aspirations and choices. It focuses on the extent to which different family units provide support, advice and information, generate role-modelling effects, and have positive and negative expectations of disabled children. It further explores how relationships with same-sex relatives and single parents influence the young people's aspirations including their choice to pursue gender-typical employment.

Chapter 2
Career Development and Choices
of Young People

Introduction

This chapter begins with a discussion about the significance of work and employment to constructions of modern adulthood, particularly in relation to disabled people. Attention is paid to the employment situation of disabled people, including how different strategies and policies over the years, particularly flexible labour markets, have influenced disabled people's employment opportunities in contemporary Britain. It moves on to discuss theoretical arguments around work and career development, exploring how young people develop occupational career choices for adulthood.

Drawing on a body of empirical evidence, including the work of Pierre Bourdieu, this analysis examines the extent to which young people's actions and decisions are culturally and socially situated, and the factors that promote or dampen career aspirations. One of these factors is disability.

The chapter debates the introduction of some special provisions that facilitate education-to-work transitions for young disabled people but devalue their employability and prolong their dependence on state benefits. It outlines the major challenges facing disabled people through their life courses at critical points of transition, and highlights the policies that have helped and hindered their transition to adulthood. In conclusion some strategies that would result in young disabled people receiving the same opportunities as their non-disabled peers in educational and labour markets are suggested.

Work, Disability and Adulthood

Participation in work and employment is a key signifier of adult status. Niles, Herr and Hartung (2001) observe that although adults have multiple roles, their occupational positions tie them to wider society by giving them a sense of purpose and identity in both work and non-work roles.

The modern experience of work has changed in response to the impact of economic, cultural, technological and organizational change. In recent years the act of working has been seen as vital, not only for financial survival, but also as a means of attaining personal satisfaction and earning a respectable position in society (Charles and James 2003; Harpaz and Fu 2002). It has been proposed as critical to the growth of people to have a healthy autonomous lifestyle (Aiken, Ferman and Sheppard 1968).

Work is an important aspect of people's everyday lives, providing access to categories of experience that are important for mental health and well-being. There is a strong relationship between unemployment and mental illness, and ill health in general leading to premature death (Bartley 1994). As Warr (1985) and Harpaz and Fu (2002) concur, work is important in that it fulfils individual roles and psychosocial needs such as a sense of being tied to society, purposefulness, self-worth, self-esteem, fulfilment, identity and status. For example, the disabled people participating in Shah's (2005a) study *Career Success of Disabled High-Flyers* saw their work as instrumental to their identity. They argued that it reduced diagnostic overshadowing in that it served to override the high-flyers' disability status that was ascribed to them as a result of medical diagnosis of their impairments. Sutherland (1981) argues that the act of working can counteract diabolism if people occupy a status that is socially prestigious and economically rewarding, and possess a university degree. This is supported by Shah (2005a) who maintains that by occupying a responsible, prestigious role in the developing economy, disabled people have a greater chance of being respected and accepted into mainstream society.

Being part of the modern labour market can have considerable social repercussions on other domains of functioning as well as personal effects (Bandura et al. 2001). For instance, in the 'Meaning of Work' (MOW) project, an eight-country comparative study conducted in the early 1980s, respondents from Japan and Yugoslavia ranked work as the most important aspect of their lives, taking precedence over family, leisure, community and religion. Dublin (1956) and Barker (1968) propose that an individual's life experiences are segmented into different sub-spheres, and that people differ in their preferences for particular life spheres. Therefore when the work sphere occupies a central or most preferred position in an individual's life, they are said to be high in career centrality.

The changing organization of society and expectations of its members means that non-work roles need not be secondary to work roles (Gerson 1993). This is supported by a study by the National Centre for Social Research (Woodland et al. 2003), which found that a high percentage of employers believe work–life balance is important to ensure high productivity and that work is of a high standard. The British economy is increasingly fuelled by ideas and a premium is placed on creativity and innovation more than the physical hours worked. Generally, flexible working is being marketed as a 'good thing' by labour market analysts, employment specialists and policy-makers (Casey, Metcalf and Millward 1997), encouraging economic growth and national economic competitiveness.

Over the past decade the growth in flexible working has arisen across large and small industries and occupations. Workplace flexibility takes many forms: flexitime, job sharing, telecommuting and moving from full-to part-time employment and back again without jeopardizing advancement. Further it comprises freelance and sub-contracted work. As a strategy for retaining valued employees, workplace flexibility may prove to be a sound business decision for employers no matter the size or industry sector. Many employers are already using flexibility as a retention tool in their workplaces on a one-to-one basis and with very few formal, institutionalized policies (Healy 2003). Fear of skills shortages provides one of the initial stimuli for considering new and different patterns of working. Employers and the government began to recognize the costs of female employees leaving the workforce because of childcare responsibilities. This added to employers' growing support for equality of opportunity in employment (Casey, Metcalf and Millward 1997). Further, flexible working patterns were introduced for people of retirement age to ease the transition from full-time employment to retirement and to ease employers' handover of responsibilities (Casey, Metcalf and Millward 1997). Woodland et al.'s (2003) study evidenced other ways in which flexible work practices benefit employers including having a positive impact on employee relations, employee commitment and labour turnover. The use of flexitime, for example, enables staff to bank extra days off but gives the employer the flexibility to extend working hours to meet vital deadlines. Further they discovered that where employers offered flexitime there was a greater level of co-operation and support between employer and employee. Flexitime allows employees to arrange appointments during time off which, in turn, helps reduce absenteeism. It can also be used to reduce the need for overtime payments.

Despite significant changes in the modern labour force (as was summarized in Chapter 1), issues such as those associated with disabled people and employment remain at the forefront of debates about equality. At age 16–17, young disabled people are approximately twice as likely to be unemployed or 'doing something else' compared with non-disabled young people. At age 18–19 they are three-times as likely to be unemployed (Burchardt 2005). According to the Labour Force Survey (2006) disabled people have a lower employment rate than any other minority group, with only around 50 per cent of disabled people of working age employed compared to 80 per cent of non-disabled people. In 2003, disabled people were the largest group of benefit claimants, accounting for around 25 per cent of all benefit expenditure (ONS 2003). Further, disabled people who are working earn 30 per cent less than non-disabled people. There are particular concerns around labour market inactivity amongst disabled young people. Disabled young people are considerably less likely than non-disabled people to be in education, employment or training, particularly from age 19 when many will first transfer out of special school (Cabinet Office 2005). The report, *Improving the Life Chances of Disabled*

People identified the need for a champion for disabled people within government. This prompted some key recommendations including establishing an Office for Disability Issues (ODI), launched on 1 December 2005, with a specific focus on improving opportunities for disabled people throughout their lives. The ODI will ensure disability policy is a priority right across government. Where services have been disjointed and presented barriers to disabled people, this office will ensure government departments work together and in partnership with disabled people to change this. The Cabinet Office report also recommended setting up a National Framework for Organizations of Disabled People (NFODP) to enable disabled people to communicate directly with the government.

'Welfare-to-work' is an important and salient public policy area, referring to policy interventions designed to promote the transition from out-of-work benefit receipt to paid employment. The 1997 New Deal for Disabled People (NDDP), part of the government's broader New Deal programme for getting all people off benefits, has put disabled people at the centre of the current UK government's 'welfare-to-work' strategy. This is a response to concerns about both the rising costs of incapacity-related benefits and calls from the disability movement to tackle poverty and exclusion (Barnes 2002; Disability Alliance 1991; DWP 2003). The NDDP incorporates two distinct elements, namely the Innovative Schemes, which include a variety of training and work placement measures, and the Personal Advisor Service (PAS), which offers one-to-one support to disabled people on locating, obtaining or remaining in employment. Evidence by Loumidis et al. (2001) shows that the PAS did, in fact, facilitate disabled people leaving benefits and also increased the rate at which this happened. For instance, over a two-year period, 11 per cent of disabled people who participated in PAS, compared to 7 per cent who did not, left benefits. However, benefit exit did not always equate to entering employment (Bambra, Whitehead and Hamilton 2005), and when it did, the quality of employment gained was perceived, by participants, to be poor (Loumidis et al. 2001).

There have been a few major welfare-to-work strategies aimed specifically at increasing labour market participation rates for disabled people and people with chronic illness (Bambra, Whitehead and Hamilton 2005). These include education, training and work placements, vocational advice and support services, in-work benefits, incentives for employers, and improving accessibility.

Welfare reform initiatives, including the Access to Work (AtW) programme, the Pathways to Work initiative and the reform of incapacity benefit are geared to helping disabled people return to the workforce or to allow employers to retain people who become disabled while in employment, thus narrowing the gap in the employment rates between disabled and non-disabled people (currently 51 per cent and 81 per cent respectively) (DRC 2006). AtW is mainly tax-funded although co-payments from employers are required in most circumstances. AtW helps with the cost of adaptations to the workplace, special equipment, personal assistance at work (for example, a reader for a blind employee), and travel to and from work. However, work experience or volunteering is not fully covered by AtW or the DDA, which hinders young disabled people's access to vocational training, and puts them at a disadvantage to their non-disabled peers.

Pathways to Work has been piloted since October 2003 for new claims in seven localities. Between October 2005 and October 2006, the pilots have been introduced everywhere, with the highest proportions of people receiving incapacity-related benefits. The Pathways package has been more effective than previous attempts to encourage people on incapacity-related benefits to participate. According to the Welfare Reform Report published by the DRC (2006), six times as many people are participating in Pathways areas compared with New Deal for Disabled People nationally. Furthermore, twice as many people have entered jobs (almost 20,000 in the seven areas in 2005).

Both the British government and European programmes put entry to the workforce at the core of their strategies to combat social exclusion. At the level of more general theory, Finkelstein has pointed out repeatedly (1980; 1993) 'that the predominant factor contributing to the disablement of different groups is the way in which people can participate in the creation of social wealth' (1993, 12). The British Council of Disabled People argues that: 'The right to a job is a fundamental Human Right' (BCODP 1996, 3). Lunt and Thornton (1994) have surveyed some of the issues involved in implementing employment policies in terms of a social model of disablement. Direct discrimination and lack of suitable educational and training opportunities have been and continue to be barriers. Just as importantly, the structure of employment has implications for disabled people. According to Jolly (2000), disabled workers are likely to endure sub-standard working conditions and they have fewer chances for promotion. Further, Abberley (1999) argues that jobs designed around the capacity, stamina and resources of the average worker – nine-to-five, five days a week employment – are damaging to the needs of a wide variety of citizens. This first became apparent in relation to women, but is equally relevant to disabled people, whatever their gender.

This changing workplace culture, with its reduction in restrictive work schedules, workplace flexibility and extended in-work support (included in the Pathways to Work package), presents new improved opportunities for disabled workers, whose successful employment was previously hampered by the traditional full-time competitive work schedule that failed to account for their reduced activity tolerance levels. The new flexible workplace facilitates disabled workers to maximize their productivity and strive towards long-term success. Further it contributes to the reduction of what the New Right call the 'dependency culture' by spending money on encouraging work rather than keeping people on benefits (Holden 1999). At the same time, organizations become better equipped with specific skills and knowledge to compete in a global labour market and to meet the needs of a diverse customer base (Cassell 1997; Dickens 1994). For example, Duckworth (1995) argues that disabled people living in a predominantly disabling world have to develop highly refined problem-solving skills that can be seen as valuable to today's economic development. However, as Stone (1984) and Priestley (1997) argue, the economic benefits of employing disabled people change in response to economic trends and demands. For example, people who are perceived as unable to work during an economic recession may be brought into the labour market during wars or periods of economic growth.

Such an analysis suggests that the definition of disability is determined by structural changes in the labour market that influence the extent to which disabled adults have opportunities to participate in the labour market. Gruber (2000 1162, 83) refers to policy definitions of disability as 'elastic', as they are more likely to be based on the actual production of profit rather than fixed biological definitions of impairment.

However, flexible working is not always the best way forward, as highlighted by Casey, Metcalf and Millward (1997). They argue that in certain organizations traditional, permanent, rather then flexible, working patterns engender high staff morale and commitment to their jobs, and low levels of staff turnover. Further many companies fear an avalanche of requests with employees dictating their hours of work, resulting in extra costs or the inability to guarantee delivery of services. Another worry with flexible working patterns is that they fundamentally shift power towards employers, while providing further opportunity for the marginalization of oppressed groups (Holden 1999). So although it is clear from the evidence above that flexible working patterns do benefit disabled people and women who need to accommodate for periods of fatigue or childcare needs, they do not seem to reduce employment inequalities. For instance, research indicates that Black unemployment rates are twice those of Whites, and even greater for particular groups. African/Caribbean men are more than three times more likely to be unemployed than White men, while Pakistani/Bangladeshi women are nearly five times as likely to be unemployed as White women (CRE 1997). Similarly, according to the Cabinet Office report (2005), only one in two disabled people are likely to be employed compared to one in four non-disabled people.

Career Choices and Development

Career development, as opposed to training for job skills, can be defined as the preparation for, choice of, entry into and adjustment to work throughout the lifespan (Super 1990). Hall (1969) argues that careers represent a way of life, an environment rather than a set of isolated work functions or skills. Individuals see their careers as part of them, structuring a large part of their everyday reality and their daily social relations. Super's life-span life-space approach to career development, introduced in the 1950s, suggests that in order to understand an individual's career, it is important to know and appreciate the web of life roles that embed the individual and his or her life concerns. Thus, the life-cycle approach addresses the individual's life situation, whilst focusing on how people change and make transitions as they prepare for, engage in, and reflect on, their life roles, especially work. Furthermore, it acknowledges that a large and complex set of factors interact dynamically in determining the choice and course of careers. As Hodkinson and Sparkes (1997) argue, career decisions are context-related and cannot be separated from the individual's family background, culture and life history. Not only are young people involved in educational and career decision-making, but they are also members of families, have friends, engage in leisure activities, and so on. All these different facets of a person's existence interweave and impinge upon each other (Jones and Wallace 1992).

The career choices some young people make could be opportunistic, based on fortuitous contacts and experiences, or indeed planned and deliberately sought out. However, this is dependent on the reflexive relationship between the individual and the culture and society in which they live. Giddens (1991) is clear that choice for some is more constrained than it is for others due to the external environmental structures that define the way we live in society. This was the case for some of the young disabled people who took part in the research described in this book. Their decisions to reject occupations they previously aspired to stemmed from educational restrictions that were beyond their control.

Therefore, when investigating the education and career-related choices of young people, the most appropriate methodology would be ethnography, which draws on the key assumption that the choice process is unique, eclectic and unpredictable. Further it is exploratory in nature, thus able to generate information about the choices young disabled people make over time, including how unpredictable turning points create new choices which may not be the same as those aspired to before, but 'occur when an individual has to take stock, to re-evaluate, revise, resee, and rejudge' (Strauss 1962, 71). As Hodkinson, Sparkes and Hodkinson (1996) argue, it is important for decision-making to be seen in the context of the life course to avoid an assumption that beyond the transition to work, an adult's future career trajectory follows predictable patterns.

Strauss (1962) claims that turning points can occur in all parts of our lives. This includes occupational careers where, according to Hodkinson (2003), a turning point is a short period when a person's career changes track. This may be as a consequence of individuals failing to match predetermined norms or a mismatch between personal motivations and official structures.

Turning points may be understood as a trigger to personal development: the beginning of an education, a job or a partnership. Hodkinson and Sparkes (1997) discern three categories of turning points. The first is structural, determined by repetition of patterns of life course that are built into the society where the person lives. Students go through one such structural turning point at the end of their compulsory schooling, when they have to decide whether to stay on to further their education full-time or leave to do vocational training. Another arises at compulsory retirement age. The next category of turning point is 'self-initiated', in that the individual concerned is instrumental in precipitating a transformation in response to a range of external factors in their personal life in the field. Finally, turning points can be caused by external factors that are either beyond a person's control or the actions of others that force individuals to reconsider their future. The latter could include debilitating accidents or illness. External turning points relevant to this research include inequalities and disabling barriers in social and economic opportunity structures that force disabled people to rethink, re-evaluate and change their aspired goals over time. For example, one young person in the research came across barriers to entering a college course necessary for her aspired career path and thus was forced to review her career goals. External turning points, caused by health, personal crisis or sudden closure of service provision, could result in disabled people undergoing 'forced' transitions (Grewal et al. 2004). According to McGinty and Fish (1992), a transition can refer to a distinct period of time or a process of personal development, so a forced transition could be conceived of as a period of personal growth that was not planned but rather caused by an accident or crisis, for instance, changes in the structure of service delivery.

When societal structures deny young disabled people the opportunity to follow their aspired choices to occupational adulthood, they are referred to as 'failed' or 'incomplete' transition cases. Idealized and individualist notions of adulthood have generated an increasing investment in special institutions concerned with 'independence' and life skills training, considered important to achieving independent adulthood. However, concerns have emerged with regard to the actual aims and functions of such inventions and their value to social inclusion. These institutions have been criticized by Priestley (2003) because their purpose is not to facilitate young disabled people to meet their career goals and increase their market value to compete with their non-disabled peers in the global labour market, but merely to manage the problems arising from failing or incomplete transitions. As Grewal et al. (2004) point out in a DWP report, some disabled people are prevented from progressing up the educational hierarchy or moving into employment due to lack of access and support in these areas. Thus they are forced to stay in these training institutions for longer periods of time than they desire. Further, the training provided in these institutions focuses on less marketable and lower status qualifications, primarily concerned with the acquisition of 'life skills' (Riddell, Baron and Wilson 2001).

The choices made during formative periods of development shape the course of our lives. Foskett and Hemsley-Brown (2001) contend that in the course of our lifetimes, the way in which we exist as people is founded on the choices we make for ourselves and of those made by others. So, the very social, cultural and economic structures within which we all operate are the products of individuals' choices over time. For Bourdieu, the French sociologist, the individual actions, beliefs and therefore the choices that create these structures must be culturally and socially situated, as all people are born into a social setting. Choice is the outcome of a process that brings together emotion, personal history, values, ideology and the implicit assumptions and aspirations of an individual's habitus (Bourdieu and Pearson 1990). Individuals act and think as a person of a particular gender, race, age or class, living in a particular period in time. Further, decision-making is part of the interaction with other stakeholders, which means that a pragmatic decision can only be understood as a part of actions of others, as well as those of the person supposedly making the choice. For instance, the choice to create special provisions of transitional support for young disabled people to undergo training in 'life skills', instead of high status qualifications that would enhance their employability, could be criticized for contributing to the disproportionate risk of unemployment and financial dependency faced by disabled people at the very time when the government is working to get people off incapacity benefit and into the labour market. Further, Kilsby and Beyer (1996) contend that in such institutions, young disabled people are less likely to have opportunities to interact socially with non-disabled peers than they would have in the world of work. Tomlinson and Colquhoun (1995) suspect that special provision puts young disabled people at a disadvantage by not sufficiently preparing them for economic participation in the declining youth labour markets of capitalist society.

Bourdieu (1977b) uses the concept *habitus* to encapsulate the ways in which a person's ideas, beliefs and preferences are individually subjective, but also influenced by the objective cultural networks and social traditions in which that person lives. Habitus not only affects the types of decisions made but how they are made.

People make career decisions within horizons for action: the arena in which actions can be taken and decisions can be made. Habitus and the opportunity structures of the labour market both influence horizons for action and are inter-related. Perceptions of what might be acceptable and appropriate affect decisions, so that opportunities are simultaneously subjective and objective (Hodkinson, Sparkes and Hodkinson 1996). Horizons both limit and present the choices people make within their world. For example, Astin (1984) recalls that while her first career choice was architecture, her dreams of becoming an architect never materialized because the social norms of the day dictated otherwise. She claims that her father saw architecture as a sub-field of his own field, engineering, which he considered to be an exclusively male field, and strongly discouraged her from pursuing it, believing it held no opportunities for women. Through habitus, horizons for action are often based on interpretations of the present made in the light of past experiences. So, Astin rejected her original aspiration as a consequence of the segmented and stratified labour market, and her father's schematic perceptions, stemming from his past experiences, of what are appropriate jobs for women. However, if Astin's life history had been different, in terms of growing up in a policy climate of gender equality in employment, and she had developed strong self-efficacy beliefs towards traditionally male career pursuits, her habitus and horizons for action would have enabled her to follow her dream.

In this book, I will explore young disabled people's horizons for action, and how they enable and restrict their career aspirations. For instance, I question how the cultures of special schools and mainstream schools influence young disabled people's future outlook. Giddens (1997) argues that education is an essential agent of socialization, required for a society to survive. Minuchin and Shapiro (1983) further argue that it is the school that provides the child with their first social arena within which they are taught to realize the consequences of social and academic competence, competition and power development. While attending educational institutions, students experience several ecological transitions that entail progressive or more drastic movements into more complex contexts. The mastery of these transitions will have a positive impact on the student's move from school to work in the future (Shah 2005b). However, in present day society the optimism that underlies the philosophy of education is somewhat frayed by the lack of facilities available to society's culturally diverse population, limiting young disabled people's horizons for action and shaping their ideas and preferences for pursuing future goals. For instance, the truncated curriculum of special schools could be responsible for young disabled people not pursuing certain career paths, thus limiting their occupational futures. However, according to Tomlinson (1982), the aim of special education was to enable disabled children to fit unobtrusively into adult society, not to facilitate them to achieve academically or to secure employment.

Youth Transitions: School-to-Work

In all societies, adolescence is a period of social transition for individuals. Over this period, society stops perceiving people as children and starts recognizing them as adults. The specific elements of the transition from childhood to adulthood vary across time and space, but many societies recognize when the individual has become socially redefined (Steinberg 2002). In Western contemporary societies like the UK, there is an expectation that children will develop consistently towards idealized goals of social and economic autonomy and independence. For non-disabled young people, this social passage is marked out by several related changes in social roles. Among the most important events in this transition is the completion of compulsory schooling, the entrance into further or higher education, becoming a full-time member of the labour market, leaving one's family (or the equivalent, such as local authority care) to set up a new, independent home, becoming involved in sexual relationships and eventually cohabiting or marrying, becoming a parent and becoming a full adult consumer, able to purchase commodities which signify adult status.

Disabled young people hope for the same things as other young people: to travel, get a good job, start a family and live independently. They want a voice, a leisure and social life, and to be involved as active, valued citizens (NOP 2003). However, they also face disabling social, attitudinal and environmental barriers that can cause disruption and anxiety, and delay or even prevent the achievement of independent living and social inclusion. As Burchardt (2005) points out, young disabled people are much less likely than their non-disabled peers to feel they have control over their futures.

Changes in economic and social policies have meant that young non-disabled people are dependent on their families for longer than before. For instance, prior to the industrial revolution children were treated as miniature adults, providing labour to their families and learning the roles they were expected to fulfil in later life (Steinberg 2002). With industrialization came new patterns of work, schooling and family life which had a dramatic influence on the transitions from childhood to adulthood. Children were unsure about what skills they needed for adulthood and consequently were more likely to stay in education to learn and prepare for the future. This was convenient for society because industrialization brought a shortage of job opportunities due to manpower being replaced by machinery. Further, industrialization brought with it changes in community life, which put young people in dangerous working environments and vulnerable to increasing crime.

The trend of young people entering the labour force later has gradually increased through the twentieth and twenty-first centuries as the workplace has continued to change in ways that make the future uncertain. Morrow and Richards (1996b) report from their study *Transitions to Adulthood: A Family Matter?*, that financially or economically, young people are technically able to leave school at the age of 16 and go into full-time work, where they may receive adult pay levels. However, some young people, including young disabled people, may face challenges in transition relating to employment, self-esteem and relationships (DCSF 2005). According to Burchardt (2005) disabled people between 16 and 26 are less satisfied with their lives and have lower social well-being than their non-disabled contemporaries. Further they do not achieve the qualifications that they could at school due to a number of factors including being exposed to negative expectations by teachers, special schools lacking an academic orientation, and a lack of education provision during hospital and other absences (Cabinet Office 2005). Disabled young people are much more likely to stay on in further education or a training centre, or to become unemployed, than get a full-time job.

As mentioned above, the government is working hard towards increasing employment opportunities for disabled adults with legislation like the DDA and schemes such as Access to Work. However, as these do not cover work experience, holiday jobs and volunteering, young disabled people lose opportunities to develop transferable life skills perceived as fundamental to personal success (Powney and Lowden 2000).

Tannock and Flocks (2003) contend that some non-disabled young people, particularly from working-class backgrounds with low educational achievement, are likely to work part-time to pay for extra tuition, evening classes, or personal and living expenses. However, most young disabled people will not have the opportunity to have part-time summer or weekend jobs, and are thus prevented not only from developing and deploying life skills, but also from covering personal expenses and contributing to the income of the family household. As paid or unpaid employment is seen as the key signifier of social inclusion in modern societies (Priestley 2003, 133), the barriers that young disabled people face to participation in either form of work contributes to their exclusion and difference:

> The struggle to achieve integration into ordinary employment is the most vital part of the struggle to change the organization of society so that physically impaired people are no longer impoverished through exclusion from full participation. Only when all physically impaired people of working age are as a matter of course helped to make whatever contribution they can in ordinary work situations, will secure foundations for full integration in society as a whole be laid. All the other situations from which physically impaired people are excluded are linked, in the final analysis, with the basic exclusion from employment. (Union of Physically Impaired Against Segregation/ Disability Alliance 1976, 15–16)

As young disabled people stay financially and socially dependent on their parents and benefits, respectively, for longer than expected, they are in danger of prolonging a dependency culture.

Young disabled people are often denied full citizenship due to the barriers in attitudes, institutions, language and culture, organization and delivery of support services, and the power relations and structures of which society is constituted (Swain et al. 2004). The complexity of a transfer from services provided to children to services provided to adults also affects many young people. There is a significant gap between children's and adults' services for disabled people. When young disabled people approach adulthood, their entitlement to services changes.

This is as a result of change in age and administrative departments, not need. The lack of coherent continuity between child and adult services may result in disabled young people being placed in residential segregated institutions due to the lack of alternative opportunities. However, models such as individualized budgets and person-centred planning have been proposed as a means of providing a seamless transition from children's to adult services for young disabled people (Cabinet Office 2005). Such models (if they were implemented properly) would empower disabled people to be independent and fulfil their roles as responsible citizens.

Researchers have argued that disabled children are perceived as vulnerable, and eternally childlike 'since their dependency has been constructed as longer lasting and qualitatively different than that of other children' (Priestley 2003, 72). Thus they are prevented from developing social skills and self-confidence because their lives are controlled by adults (Alderson and Goodey 1998; Morris 1997; Norwich 1997). As a result of close adult surveillance and inaccessible environments, a disabled child is likely to experience neither a normal childhood, nor adolescence, and is likely to be conditioned into an adulthood of dependency (Middleton 2003). This experience may be illustrated by the following quotation:

> As a child I was never left alone apart from bedtime. I wanted to be left alone. Even going to the toilet somebody had to sit me on the toilet and wait for me to get off. That scared me because I didn't want people round me all the time. (Middleton 2003, 2)

Such over-protectiveness of disabled children can have fatal consequences for them when trying to make sense of adulthood. Middleton (2003) maintained that the lack of choice and control experienced by young disabled people from an early age can stifle their transitions to independent adulthood. For example, they can either become overeager to please and lose the ability to think for themselves, or start challenging everything. A further difficulty for disabled children who have been protected and segregated from the mainstream world is the ability to form relationships with non-disabled people and indeed vice versa. Shah (2005a) suggests that inclusion can (for some people) facilitate the establishment of social relationships between disabled and non-disabled peers, as awareness and understanding of disability is said to engender an increasing acceptance of it. Young disabled people may experience feelings of isolation in adulthood and lack the self-confidence to build up relationships in mainstream environments. There is also a danger of them becoming crushed by trauma because they have always been controlled by others and had decisions made for them. Thomas (1998) found that some disabled women who spent long periods of their childhood in hospital, at a time when parents were kept out of the wards except for brief visits, were left with lasting fears of separation and a strong sense of insecurity.

However, this is not necessarily always the case, as evidenced in Shah's (2005a) study of disabled high-flyers. It showed that children who receive a lot of parental affection and attention, and have their needs gratified quickly, feel secure and are more likely to explore and move towards independence. Further the study found that a supportive upbringing, which encouraged personal internal locus of control and a strong need to achieve, helped disabled people to survive early adverse experiences. This in turn led to a basic feeling of strength, independence, self-sufficiency, responsibility and an early sense of mastery. Development of these traits was critical to successful transitions to adulthood.

Despite the handful of success stories including those highlighted by Shah (2005a), the reality is that all too often disabled children are denied opportunities to make their own choices and make transitions that meet their own goals. This could be due to physical and social barriers embedded in societal structures, examples of which are illustrated in this book. It could also be due to the fact that the focus of policy and practice is on incapacity and inability rather than giving disabled children opportunities to develop the life skills necessary to successfully follow the social passage to adulthood. This, however, is not dissimilar to the situation of some non-disabled young people (mentioned earlier) who stay with and remain financially dependent on their families because they have problems of adjustment – socially, vocationally and into adulthood.

Given this, a life-skills instruction approach could be part of every school curriculum, alongside more traditional subjects. This would teach disabled and non-disabled young people key transferable skills necessary for independent adulthood, which would increase rather than decrease young people's market value and employability. Further it would not be conceived as a way of dealing with failed transitions (Priestley 2003) or a special provision for young disabled people who cannot achieve their aspirations, but an inclusive approach fundamental to the occupational futures of all young people.

However, adopting such an inclusive approach in education is not enough to guarantee young disabled people's equal participation in the labour market. As Barnes, Thornton and Maynard Campbell (1998) argue, many young disabled people are unable to access mainstream employment schemes because of a lack of specialized facilities, learning materials and on-site personal care and support. Further, recent research has indicated that employers varied in terms of their understanding of the needs of disabled people and the definitions of disability, with employers who were less experienced at recruiting and employing disabled people tending to take a much narrower view (Aston et al. 2005). Aston et al. found that when employers did recruit disabled people it was usually to low-level semi-skilled or light manual work. They suggest that employers increasingly made physical adjustments to the workplace after the introduction of the New Deal for Disabled People (NDDP), but they also perceived adverse financial consequences and a high sickness rate as constraints to employing disabled people. However, adjustments do not cost much at all, and indeed some are free. According to a report by the Disability Rights Commission (2001), two-thirds of the changes needed to accommodate people in the workplace cost nothing, and the remainder £76 per person. Furthermore, there is no evidence to suggest that all disabled people are less productive than non-disabled people. Ensuring that the right people are in the right roles with the right support is the important thing, rather than making negative assumptions and excluding potential talent (Disability Rights Commission 2005).

The need for effective training and support for young disabled people generated a new employment initiative in Northern Ireland called Vocational Opportunities in Training for Employment (VOTE). The two-year pilot experienced considerable success in that it facilitated some young disabled people to access mainstream college courses and enter the 'real' world of work (Taylor, McGilloway and Donnelly 2004). Unlike some transition institutions for young disabled people, VOTE was seen as a stepping stone rather than a permanent feature of life. Gerber, Reiff and Ginsberg 1996) considered this helped young disabled people reframe their view of the world and their impairment as part of a mental preparation for working life. A further important aspect of VOTE is that it encouraged social interaction between disabled and non-disabled people, in preparation for transition to adulthood. However, the effectiveness of such initiatives as VOTE can only be sustained if specialized employment training and support are integrated with mainstream employment or training services. This, coupled with the aforementioned inclusive approach in education, could significantly improve the employment situation of young disabled people.

A similar initiative that has proved successful in terms of increasing the employment rate of young disabled people is the Residential Training Scheme, one of the New Deal Innovative Schemes. It used 14 specialist training colleges in the UK to provide extensive one-year courses, sometimes leading to vocational qualifications, for disabled people. Maton et al.'s (2000) analysis indicated that employment rates for disabled people who participated rose by 43 per cent after one month of attending, and to 50 per cent after 18 months. The study also showed that disabled students believed it had increased their employment opportunities and the level of employment they could attain.

Conclusion

The discussion in this chapter confirms the importance of employment in the social and economic lives of adults and young people. Further it highlights the existence of systematic inequalities between people with and without impairments in the labour market, and the recent policy initiatives that have been introduced to address these. However, while the government develops and implements strategies to increase disabled people's participation in the mainstream labour market, they have also introduced major social institutions to manage the problems arising from failed transitions. The chapter has explored how this contributes to the exclusion of young disabled people, devalues their employability and prolongs their dependence on state benefits. It offers suggestions of possible supports for young disabled people to obtain equal training to their non-disabled peers so they can go to work and share their expertise in a global economy.

Chapter 3

Young People's Aspirations: What Are They and Why?

Introduction

This chapter begins with a summary of career development theories and a discussion about choices, particularly occupational decision-making and the significance of age and maturity level. It explores why some young people make wide-ranging choices while those of others are more specific. The chapter moves on to examine how young people's choices are constructed, discussing the constraints of personal factors such as gender, impairment, ability, family background, social class, and social and political structures. Along with this it is concerned with the extent to which policy change in labour and educational markets serves to dictate the career-related choices people make. It discusses the issue of employment constraints and penalties in the labour market, taking women and people from ethnic minorities as examples of how changing labour markets determine employment opportunities, thus indicating how choices are socially situated. Disabled people are another group whose choices and opportunities are determined somewhat by social and political structures and practices. The question is how much young disabled people's choices are driven by the situations they themselves and the people in their lives, are in, and how much is about their own desires, interests and ability levels. The degree to which young disabled people's aspirations and trajectories are constrained and shaped by social structures and/or agency is highlighted by the young disabled people's stories. By integrating the theory with young disabled people's narratives about their aspired goals, including what they were, why they were chosen, how they could be achieved and the barriers anticipated to successful goal achievement, this chapter explores the extent to which the young disabled people's aspirations were clearly defined or wide ranging, and the reasons behind this, including the influence of age and individual interpretation of disability and impairment. Further, it examines goals that the young people had to reject or redirect, and their views about this experience. In this chapter there is an emphasis on listening to young disabled people about what they want and the barriers they encountered when trying to meet aspired goals. Through their voices, they reveal the social structures that contribute to the inequalities they face in society, and how these have restricted their choices, opportunities and trajectories. Further, the mechanisms for choice and change identified will lessen inequalities and the penalties experienced by disadvantaged groups in the education and employment markets.

Young People's Development of Choices

Choices are the building blocks of structures in society. They are significant to the ways in which social structures interact with each other on a day-to-day basis and over the life course. Further, the choices made by individuals over time determine the changes to social, economic and cultural environments in the world in which they live, and the opportunities available to them at particular points in time. Although people are the products of their own choices, many of these are either facilitated or constrained by external environmental structures that define an individual's role in society (Foskett and Hemsley-Brown 2001). According to Bourdieu (1977a), all individuals are born into a social setting, therefore their actions and beliefs must always be culturally and socially situated.

Ginsberg et al.'s (1951) development theory and Bandura's (1977) social learning theory, which formed the basis of Lent, Brown and Hackett's social cognitive career theory, developed in 1987, retain a strong sense in which it is the individual who determines and controls their choice outcomes.

Ginsberg's development theory presents occupational choice as an unfolding, maturational process whereby an individual progresses through three stages (fantasy, tentative and realistic), to the point where they can make realistic choices. In the fantasy stage (before age 11), the child is free to pursue any occupational choice, believing they can become whatever they want to. Through this process the child's preferred activities are identified, and they make arbitrary translations of their needs that are then related to future career choices. At this point, their choices are still broad and wide-ranging. The connection between age and the extent to which the young people's goals were defined was evident from the young people's narratives. Hannah, aged 18, mentioned her childhood ambition to be a singer was actually a dream:

> I used to want to be a singer. Which wasn't going to happen, but it was a big dream of mine ... I lost my confidence as well. I used to be able to sing in front of anyone, but, since I got older I just stopped.

She rejected her aspiration as a consequence of growing up, or according to Ginsberg et al.'s development theory (1951), growing out of the fantasy stage, becoming aware of her individual qualities and matching these to occupational options.

Several young disabled people, aged 15–17, had a clear idea of the shape they wanted their occupational future to take. This included Mike, aged 15, from a mainstream school:

> I've always wanted to go into journalism, more than that I've always wanted to go over to writing books, but journalism's just like a back-up career.

However, other young people were less sure and were still considering a wide range of goals. Both Joe and Tim, who went to the same mainstream school, expressed an interest in following a range of goals:

> I'd like to be a coach driver ... Or probably making [xxx] music for someone ... I would like to live in my own house. (Tim, aged 15)

> I want to work with my dad, fixing people's heaters ... I wanted to be a teacher ... I wanted to be a PE teacher. (Joe, aged 13)

This study found, on the whole, that two-thirds of young people had clearly defined goals, and one-third expressed wide-ranging goals. Young people expressing the former were aged 14 and over, and for the latter they were aged 15 years and under. The findings show that no 13-year-olds had clearly defined goals, and no young people aged 16 and over had wide-ranging goals. However, the fourteen young people within the 14–15 age band were divided in terms of their decision-making. Eight of them (seven from mainstream school, one from special school) had clearly defined goals, and six (four from mainstream school, two from special school) had wide-ranging goals.

Among those with clearly defined goals, most expressed an understanding of the requirements to reach their goals. For example, Tommo, aged 15, who expressed a desire to be a sports assistant, thought he needed: 'like good like umm A to C grades for like urrm a sport assistant and that you need about a good two years of training'. Hannah, aged 18, considered the specifications of a fashion photographer as being: '... a good imagination for one. I think you need to be confident, and be able to talk to people. I'd say I have these.' Sabrina, who was one of the 14-year-olds with clearly defined goals in mainstream school, wanted to be a language interpreter which, she believed, required skills such as 'good communication 'cos you can't go and talk without'. Noalga was the only young person based in special school and from the 14–15 age band, who had clearly defined goals. This could be explained by the fact that he had spent previous years in mainstream school. He talked about following a career in multimedia, and to do this he thought he would 'need ICT qualifications and skills to look on the internet'.

Although young people aged 13 years had wide-ranging goals, this did not necessarily mean all of them lacked understanding of how to reach these. Joe, who mentioned wanting to be a plumber or a PE teacher, thought he would need the following: '[for a plumber] I pick up the phone and say "hello Prickle stores" and I write things down ... All you need is a screw driver if things are leaking need mending ... [For a PE teacher] You need a, a whistle and a office key, and the boys changing room keys around your neck.' Xavier was considering either reviewing computer games for a magazine or working in a computer games shop, so, unlike Joe, his aspirations were in a particular area. When asked what he thought was required to do these jobs, he said: 'I think I definitely need English because of like writing the review, I definitely think you'd need maths for doing the till, um, computers 'cos you might be working on a computer at the shop.'

However, other young people, aged 13 or over, were not sure what was required for them to pursue their goals. They either responded to this question with a shrug, shook their heads or attempted an answer and then gave up. For example, Allan wanted to work with computer games, although he was unsure what skills might be required to do this: '... something to do with IT, technology, not sure really'. Millie mentioned a few options, although like Xavier, they were all in the same field: 'I've got quite a few choices. I've got dance choreographer, and a singer or an actress.' However, she believed that whatever goal she chose she needed 'good grades to get a good job'.

Realistic, Compromised and Rejected Goals

Among the young people with clearly defined goals, some had identified, considered or encountered potential barriers associated with these goals. This had helped them narrow down and develop their aspirations based on their ability levels. Steve and Tommo both had to reject original aspirations as a consequence of self-occupation incongruence, but narrowed their goals to jobs within their ability levels in the same occupational field as originally chosen. Steve had a keen interest in the English language, and considered following a career path in journalism: 'I did look at journalism quite seriously for a while.' However, he rejected journalism as he perceived that certain barriers associated with his impairment would prevent him from meeting the specifications of the job: 'There's a lot of pressure and speed and things to have to go into journalism I think, and speed isn't one of my best qualities.' Thus he chose to become a freelance writer instead, perceiving an occupation in journalism to be outside his horizon for action.

Tommo's favourite subjects at school were sports and biology. This triggered his original aspiration to be a physiotherapist. However, he rejected this idea as he became aware that disabling barriers might prevent him from performing certain parts of the job: 'but like some of the exercises you have to show people I struggle doing them anyway'. So, in the light of this, he changed his career goal slightly to become a sports assistant, which required similar skills and knowledge to physiotherapy. So although Tommo might not be able to perform the job he originally aspired to, he could do another job in the same field.

Beginning in the preteen years (between 11 and 17) and continuing through senior school, the young person further defines their interest in, capacity for and values with regard to an occupation. During this phase, choice factors are almost exclusively subjective but these choices are considered tentative because young people have not yet adequately considered and incorporated reality factors. For instance, how do the young people's subjective interests and capacities fit against their social class, gender or impairment? The cumulative effect is a transition process in which the adolescent recognizes the consequences and responsibility of their choice.

The realistic stage, spanning from mid-adolescence through young adulthood, allows young people to work out a compromise between their interests, capacities and values, and the opportunity structures created by their environment. The realistic period begins with the exploration stage where the young person seeks to explore the alternatives for the last time. This is proceeded by the crystallization stage where a choice is determined. Feldman (2004) contends that young disabled people may experience delays during this stage because they are less likely than non-disabled peers to participate in part-time work during teenage years and thus can face greater hurdles in testing their skills and abilities in real-world work settings.

The final stage in Ginsberg et al.'s development process is the specification stage, which sets boundaries to certain choices, and young people are guided to pursue specific social and educational experiences to successfully achieve their goals. As mentioned above, in this study a number of young people had to compromise their own aspirations, based on subjective interests, due to the limited opportunity structures available to them in disabling mainstream society. This set boundaries to some choices and accessible routes to alternative ones. For example, Fiona chose to do photography after being forced to reject her original aspiration to be a beautician as a result of disabling barriers put up by the mainstream college she had applied to. Sally also had to reject aspirations because of disabling barriers within social structures key to her transitions. Although she mentioned technology/computing as her choice (at the time of the interview), she initially had more feminine aspirations to be a hairdresser or health and social care worker. However, Sally rejected the 'hairdresser' aspiration as she became more aware of the incongruence of her own physical abilities and what she considered would be required of her as a hairdresser: 'I wanted to do hairdressing, for a bit, but like I can't do that 'cos I can't stand, well I can stand up, but I can't like stand up and then do the person's hair, you know.' After this, Sally wanted to do a course in health and social care, but this was blocked by the advice of a careers advisor who considered her impairment would make it difficult to do what was required in the curriculum:

Well I told her that I wanted to do health and social care but now I'm not doing that because I think it's lifting around and I can't really lift that much, and then um, now I'm doing dance, drama um, but I did tell her that I want to do health and social care ... she don't think I would be able to do that or something and I didn't think I'd be able to do that 'cos it's lifting and it's pushing and she told me to go away and think about it.

So Sally took the advice of a Connexions worker who persuaded her to follow a course in information technology, suggesting that this would be more suitable for someone with an impairment like Sally's.

On a similar note, Bella, who had clearly defined goals, had encountered barriers to pursuing her original aspiration to become a nurse. It could be argued that, as a disabled person, Bella would have had the qualities and dimension of knowledge needed by nurses. However, as Bella grew older she became aware of how being deaf and society's reaction to it may be a barrier to pursuing an occupation in nursing: ''cos I thought if I do it in a surgery it's a bit hard isn't it, but it's more hard doing it out of work, going round people's houses'. So although Bella did not mention any particular individual who influenced her dismissal of her original aspiration to become a nurse, it can be argued that societal ideologies of the nursing profession, coupled with the fact that the fitness standards by which nursing applicants are assessed, may pose challenges to disabled people entering and progressing in this area (DRC 2006). So, as for Fiona, Bella's choices were constrained by social structures. Despite this reality, in a society where medical interpretations of disability prevail, the problem was still considered to be with the young person's impairment and their inability to access the work, not society's failure to make the jobs accessible to their physical needs.

The barriers encountered by Bella and several of the other young people with clearly defined goals had assisted them in narrowing down their choices and developing their goals based on their perceived ability. However, their subsequent aspirations, considered to have fewer barriers, were for slightly different jobs in the same occupational field as the young people had originally aspired to, thus still tied in with their skills and interests: 'now I want to work with deaf people 'cos my mum's friend's deaf so but that's not the only reason why though. I just like working with people with disabilities it makes me feel good 'cos I help them help, as well as them helping me' (Bella).

From the empirical evidence above, it can be argued that the segmented labour market and society's portrayal of certain occupations and people with impairments can limit the kinds of careers disabled people aspire to. So, in a sense, the young people's choices were filtered by society's norms and their situations were analysed from a medical model perspective. The young disabled people were perceived to have a problem which would prevent them from meeting their aspired job or the necessary associated educational requirements. However, from a social model perspective, none of their choices were unrealistic and could have been achieved with reasonable adjustments, work rescheduling and lateral thinking. This thinking was shared by one of the Special Educational Needs Co-ordinators interviewed for this study. His attitude, unfortunately, was not that common among the educational professionals in either mainstream or special schools and, possibly, was influenced by his personal experience of impairment and disability:

> My wife is a drama teacher who has had a congenital hip problem since birth. It doesn't stop her teaching it, she may not be able to run around like everybody else but it doesn't stop her. Especially nowadays where everything is supposed to be adapted in the workplace ... I would encourage anyone to do anything. I teach special needs kids. I tell them 'you can do what you want, it might take a bit longer, it took me 27 years to become a teacher'. If you are a kid with NHS glasses and epilepsy, you don't have confidence – but I still got there and it's the same for them – they might not be able to go at the same speed as everyone else but they can still get there.

Lent, Brown and Hackett's 1987 social cognitive career theory (SCCT) proposes that career choice is influenced by the beliefs the individual develops and refines through four major sources: a) personal performance accomplishments, b) vicarious learning, c) social persuasion and d) physiological states and reactions. SCCT places an emphasis on the mechanisms used to shape and mould interests. As individuals try activities and receive feedback on their performance, they develop self-efficacy and outcome expectations about the activities. If, as a result of positive feedback or self-evaluation, individuals become competent and expert at a particular activity, their self-efficacy or belief that they have the ability to execute the relevant behaviour to succeed in a given task, is reinforced. Repeated successes demonstrate that they are more likely to be as a consequence of internal forces such as ability rather than luck or significant others. This is likely to increase young people's self-esteem and choice in pursuing specific goals involving continual engagement with the particular activity. At this stage individuals have the confidence to develop strategies to combat perceived barriers (Hill, Ramirez and Dumka 2003). Individuals who perceive challenges or barriers to achieving success in certain activities, and have no evidence that they are able to overcome these barriers, are more likely to have low self-efficacy beliefs and wide-ranging goals.

SCCT acknowledges the importance of contextual factors in terms of influencing the extent to which the individual perceives the probability of success. For instance, young people from low-income families are less likely than those from more affluent families, to be expected to aspire to high-status occupations (Conger et al. 1993; McLoyd 1989). This may be due to the fact that the latter are less likely to have access to information about options available and how to qualify for occupations. Like socio-economic factors, ethnic minority status, disabling society and conceptions of impairment and gender, socialization may increase or limit young people's career-related aspirations in terms of what occupations they perceive are available to them (Arbona 1989; Barnes and Mercer 2005; Swanson and Woike 1997). As Hodkinson, Sparkes and Hodkinson (1996) contend, the horizon for action for any individual is limited to a segment of the education and labour market; thus no one considers the whole range of possible opportunities, rather a limited range of jobs or careers. However, personal perceptions shaped by subcultures, highlighted above as class, gender and disability, affect the types of jobs young people are prepared to consider. Further, social structures such as school have been seen to have an impact on young people's horizons for action and limit opportunities to generate possible career goals in terms of curriculum offered, teachers' expectations of young people, work experience, quality of teaching and institutional culture (Foskett, Dyke and Maringe 2004). Conversations with some educational professionals in the current study evidenced ways in which the structures in some mainstream schools hindered disabled students' opportunities to be involved in school field trips with their fellow non-disabled peers, thus limiting potential opportunities for disabled and non-disabled peers to be inspired by new experiences, environments and relationships: 'We run trips to foreign places. In principle all can go but in practice we look very carefully at who can go with the child. There could be difficulties on health and safety grounds' (Deputy Head Teacher, mainstream school).

However, some educationalists believed that other structures, such as teaching assistants, have significantly contributed to the inclusion of young disabled people in mainstream schools: '… without them the students wouldn't get included. They can't be included if a teaching assistant isn't there to provide the personal care' (SENCO, mainstream school). This view was not always shared by young disabled people, who, in the next chapter, express different perceptions of teaching assistants.

Development of Choices – Interplay between Social and Individual Factors

Although the career development theories discussed do acknowledge the influence of social and cultural environments on decision-making, these are not perceived as integral to the process itself. For instance, individuals' interests, capacities and values are all simultaneously objective and subjective. Individuals develop them within the opportunity structures available to them. According to Hodkinson and Sparkes (1997) opportunities are not 'just out there' waiting to be chosen; young people make their choices within the context in which they are culturally and socially situated (in Bourdieu's term, their 'horizon for action'), and their economic situations in society. For example, the introduction and rapid growth of technology and improved labour productivity have caused jobs in manufacturing to decline since the 1950s. At the same time service sector jobs are on the increase (Roberts 1995). As a consequence of these changing market demands, educational and training options change. A further example is the process of schooling, which may be different for young people in different sub-cultures.

The young disabled people interviewed for this book had experiences of special school and mainstream school which had different priorities, foci, opportunity structures and philosophies. They had different perceptions: choices and the ways they made decisions were inseparable from the culture of the school they attended. So although the young disabled people's personal preferences could be exercised, and they did make different choices, these were to some extent shaped by the needs of society and the economy. From this, one can argue that choices and opportunities are both subjective and objective because what is available, what is perceived to be possible, and what is perceived as desirable can alter the range of 'available' options (Wright 2005). This can be demonstrated by the case of Tyson and Mike. Tyson, a 19-year-old girl, based in special school, expressed a keen interest in drama as a possible area to work in the future. Her choice was influenced by the resources made available through school networks, coupled with her personal interest in the area and the fact she believed she was good at it: 'I led drama workshops in Hungary, so I've done some leading in my time ... I have actually done a drama course on Saturday mornings ... one of the teachers who's left now, he got connections that's how I got to know about it.' Mike's aspiration to be a journalist was influenced by his interest in reading fiction, his love of and success in running the school magazine, and his ability to write for an audience:

> I run the school magazine. I like reading magazines, so I thought, because there's only one magazine at school I thought I'd start my own. I've done that, I've done that but I've always wanted to go into journalism 'cos I read magazines and newspapers and stuff and I've always wanted to like write my own articles and that, but, more than that I've always wanted to go over to writing books ... my favourite author Jacqueline Wilson I went to see her on Tuesday and her experience as a writer was really good and I write to her a lot, well I used to, so, but just reading books I've always wanted to like be a part of writing books, just to experience what other authors go through.

Further, his experiences of disability discrimination on several occasions, which included 'one boy who was messing about with my wheelchair so I had to stop going to that class for a bit, 'cos he was like a bully, so now I wouldn't go back', motivated his desire to want to change things by writing articles for newspapers or magazines about 'the problems disabled people face and, um what can be done about it and um how people should like realize what it's like and not be horrible'.

However, Mike's own perceptions were also notably influenced by social structures and the resources they made available to him. He was well aware that having a physical impairment, resulting in the permanent use of a powered wheelchair, reduced his employment opportunities in a disabling society, so chose something that could be within his horizon for action:

> Access might be a problem. My teacher said when you start off your career they give you like court cases and well, I know courts have stairs I don't know about ramps but I know they have stairs, so access could be a big problem, and maybe writing 'cos they say it dead fast ... the writing problem I'd say I could use my laptop, I could use that but the access problem I'm not sure if there is ramps and stuff built, but I think that should be done anyway.

A number of studies concerned with the decision-making of young people (see, for instance Ball, Maguire and Macrae 2000; Hodkinson, Sparkes and Hodkinson 1996) have identified three key elements to be pragmatically rational. First, the decision-making process is part of a wider choice of lifestyle (influenced by social context and culture). Second, decision-making is part of a progressing life course, so decisions made by young people in the present are part of an ongoing course of trajectories and transitions over their lifetime. Third, decision-making evolves through interactions with others, so decisions are in fact the outcome of relationships between young people, employers, service providers, parents and so on. This again can be exemplified by the experiences of several young disabled people in the current study. Tyson's involvement in the Saturday morning drama workshops were cut short by family issues and lack of support provision for her to be able to attend the workshops regularly:

> I actually started leading group activities just before I left ... But I left due to mum's health, that's what I left for ... it was too much commitment on a Saturday morning ... My mum is basically getting old. Right with her having cancer at a very like difficult point in my life, it's like, it's really saying, my mum's not been as strong since she had the cancer. So that's been evident this past couple of years, because she is not coping.

Zoë, Schumacher and Bella had also experienced challenges as a consequence of their choices. They experienced barriers and attitudinal discrimination from non-disabled adults who were significant to their trajectories. Both Zoë and Schumacher enjoyed helping look after children, which triggered their aspiration to work as nannies or child minders, and Bella wanted to be a nurse. However, various people blocked their paths, considering their aspirations unrealistic, given the nature of their impairment: 'Mum thinks I'm living in a dream world' (Zoë, aged 17). 'Sometimes I have problems because some people look at me and think WHEELCHAIR. They think "you can't take care of my kids, you can hardly look after yourself"' (Schumacher, aged 20).

Opportunities can open up new choices, for example, when young people, teachers or parents use their local contacts to arrange work experience placements. Choices are developed from what an individual knows about the world and constrained by where they are placed within it. Individuals' interpretations of their present world and horizons for action are often made in the light of past experiences, for example, in education or the labour market, or the historical understanding of sub-groups. Further, they are influenced by structural and cultural factors that play a substantial part in developing individuals' horizons for action by influencing the resources available to them and their allies. For instance, the structural segmentation of the education and labour market, coupled with divisions of sub-cultures based on gender, ethnicity, social class and disability, shape individuals' life chances. In this way, structural/cultural factors permeate the networks young people can access, both creating opportunities to make some career choices, and limiting the choices to make others. This can be illustrated by the case studies used in Hodkinson, Sparkes and Hodkinson's (1996) investigation *Triumphs and Tears* of two working-class young men who may have had the ability, skills and intelligence to work as nannies with young children, but would have been prevented from entering such a traditionally female occupation as a consequence of their culturally grounded horizons for action. Bates and Riseborough (1993) confirm that deep-seated inequalities exist in the British labour market, which are influenced by several factors. Firstly, entry into different career trajectories is largely dependent on the level of qualifications at 16+, which are strongly influenced by social class. In the current study, Mike's school used their networks to organize work experience for him in a public library and this fed his original aspiration. However, their failure to provide accessible transport might have constrained this opportunity without the support and resourcefulness of Mike's family network:

> I did work experience in May um I did it at [library near school] ... There's a teacher, Mrs [W] special needs she sorts it out the placement and the transport and stuff and then that's it I just do all the work, get there, but when I went that time school couldn't organize transport, and it was a 40-minute walk from my house so my dad had to take me and my mum picked me up.

Gender and ethnicity also have a strong influence on employment variation and restricted opportunities in certain types of occupation. Heath and Cheung (2006), in a recent study for the Department of Work and Pensions, report that overall a number of ethnic minority groups experience lower employment rates than their White counterparts. For instance, during 2001–2004 around 62 per cent of Bangladeshi and 69 per cent of Pakistani men were economically active, compared with 85 per cent of British men. Although other ethnic groups have higher labour market participation rates, these still tend to be lower than those of the White British

(Berthoud 2000; 2002; Strategy Unit 2003). Further, ethnic minority groups tend to be concentrated in low-skilled semi-routine jobs and experience lower wage levels than White British colleagues. These disadvantages have been termed ethnic penalties (Heath and Cheung 2006), as they put ethnic minority group members at a substantial disadvantage compared to White British contemporaries. Possible explanations for ethnic penalties include discrimination, lack of information about job opportunities and poor schooling as a consequence of living in disadvantaged neighbourhoods. These inequalities all have an influence on young people's life choices, chances and trajectories.

Gender has frequently been cited as a factor in career and subject choice (Griffin 1985; Labour Force Survey 2006; Leckey, McGuigan and Harrison 1995; Marini et al. 1996). Hoffman (1972) suggests that boys and girls enter the world with different constitutional make-ups. Evidence shows that this difference is reinforced by the way society treats and speaks to children and teaches them acceptable patterns of behaviour and social roles, in accordance with their gender. Prescribed gender role behaviours that dominated in the first part of this century continue to hold the power to bias education and research, and to restrict the psychological and life choices of girls and boys, men and women (Kerr 2000). Choices thus are exercised within the restricted options imposed on them by their social position. Women do not necessarily have the choice to be a main earner in the family. They are more likely to follow their male partner to his job than to have him follow her. Further, women are more likely to have major child-rearing responsibilities. It is now the norm for women to combine work with family responsibilities but they continue to be more likely to give up full-time for part-time work, and to give up professional work, than their male contemporaries (Kerr 1997). A paper by Berthoud and Blekesaune (2006) analysed the employment penalties of different social groups, showing that while fatherhood had no effect on men's employment rates, women's employment rates were very sensitive to motherhood. Mothers are victims of higher employment penalties, again, because their own choices are constrained by the available employment opportunities with flexible hours.

Bynner, Ferri and Shepherd (1997) found significant gender differences in self-reported skills, pointing towards different sectors of the labour market, which they argue may explain why men and women continue to pursue different types of jobs. According to Kerr and Erb (1991), men are likely to disregard their own career and educational interests on the basis of gender-related ideologies. They contend that even where young people have certain interests in school and college, the majority are unlikely to pursue these interests further if they contradict societal gender norms. For instance, young men who are interested in the arts, languages and nursing while in compulsory education are less inclined to carry these forward as career goals for fear that significant others do not conceive them as lucrative or manly enough. In a study about young people's perceptions towards nursing as a career, Foskett and Hemsley-Brown (1999) report that boys aged 15–17 still perceived nursing as primarily female work and males who entered that occupation as 'gay'. Banks et al. (1992) argue that a combination of self-selection and social selection causes males and females to head for different labour segments and different types of training experiences. Hodkinson, Sparkes and Hodkinson (1996) found that by the end of their longitudinal study of participants in the Training Credit scheme, all young people whose trajectories had been tracked had chosen occupations within traditional gender-stereotypical roles. Even in cases where they started a placement in a gender-atypical job, challenges and difficulties generated by structural/cultural influences caused them to move to more traditional careers, according to gender perceptions.

This chapter suggests that gender indeed has an influence on young disabled people's career goals, despite the stereotypical notion that people with impairments are one dimensional and do not have a gender identity. In the current study, the career goals mentioned by the young disabled people as potential careers reflected the following categories from the 2005 Labour Force Survey classifications: Technology/Computing (for example, web designer, programmer, multimedia specialist), Arts/Media (for example, photographer, actor, dancer, journalist, singer), Health Care/Social Welfare Worker (for example, nanny, midwife, specialist youth worker), Sports (for example, sports assistant, basketball player), Sales/Administration (for example, box office worker, shop assistant, receptionist), Construction (for example, joiner, carpenter, painter and decorator), Education (for example, nursery teacher, language interpreter, PE teacher), and Transport (for example, coach driver). A few of the young people also mentioned the desire to live independently.

Although both boys and girls aspired to jobs within the fields of arts and media, further analysis indicated that girls were more likely to choose careers considered, by societal ideologies and national labour force statistics (Labour Force Survey 2006), as typically female, such as a singer, dancer or actress. Of the girls with aspirations within arts and media, half chose gender-typical careers. For example, Checka, Millie, Jane and Jenny expressed similar interests to pursue a career in some kind of performing arts. The girls had experienced previous success in activities relating to their aspiration, which increased their self-efficacy beliefs and need to continue engaging with such activities to pursue their goal:

I've got quite a few choices. I've got dance choreographer, and a singer or an actress. Drama's my favourite subject I think I'm quite good at drama. (Millie, aged 13)

I want to go to a performing arts college to do acting and singing ... My favourite subjects are dance and drama ... I have always wanted to do singing since I was really little. (Jenny, aged 14)

I know I want to do something to do with drama ... I'm a good little actress. (Jane, aged 18)

Strong (1943) and others suggest that there is a strong correlation between job satisfaction and interest. Also well-being criteria such as life satisfaction, self-image and self-esteem are all positively related to Person–Environment (P–E) interest congruence, that is the match between an individual's measured interests and those required for their working environment (Hansen 2005). Further, P–E congruence is related to persistence, success and performance in the job or school. Combining interests and abilities tends to improve performance in work or academic settings beyond levels that can be achieved using one construct alone (McHenry et al. 1990). This supports Strong (1943), who contends that while people with ability and interests do well in their chosen field, some people with just ability and no interests can do well, but others may not.

The career category of Technology/Computing was mentioned by just under one-third of young people in special and mainstream schools and was the second most popular occupational field. Overall more boys than girls expressed an interest in these careers. Other gender differences were apparent in the analysis of career selection. More boys were interested in pursuing employment in fields of transport and sport. More girls than boys were keen to follow careers in fields of health and social care.

So, from the above evidence it is obvious that structural inequalities greatly influence the extent to which the labour market becomes segmented and also determine individuals' life chances, encouraging people to follow prescribed paths, with a risk of compromising personal interests along the way. Given this evidence, one might question the belief in free individual choice embedded in current policy.

The consequence of choice, whether free or constrained, is different for each individual as it is shaped by highly individual facets including personal life history, life experiences, interpretations and impressions of implicit and explicit socio-cultural and economic pressures (Foskett and Hemsley-Brown 2001). So, in this respect, people are both the masters and the victims of choice. Their life courses are shaped by a combination of individual preferences, inter-linked routines and opportunity structures in a way that incorporates serendipity.

Like gender, disablement refers to socially constructed aspects of people's experiences and shapes the learning opportunities to which particular individuals are exposed, the interpersonal reactions (such as support and indifference) they receive for performing certain activities, and the future outcomes they come to anticipate (Shah 2005a). As Priestley (2003) has suggested, these are also influenced by structural changes in the political economy. Stone (1984) argues that the definition of who is included in the category of disabled people flows directly from state efforts to control the adult labour supply in market economies. So while many disabled people have historically been victims of labour market exclusion, this trend is dependent on changes in supply and demand in economic society. Barnes and Mercer (2005) have noted that the level of exclusion from paid employment exhibits some extraordinary short-term fluctuations. For instance, during the Second World War nearly half a million disabled people were called to participate in the British labour force (Humphries and Gordon 1992).

However, in most cases disabled people's horizons for action are much more limited than that of their non-disabled counterparts as a consequence of disabling barriers in society that affect the life expectations and life chances of disabled people even before they are born. In some sense, the life chances of disabled people, and indeed their horizons for action, are strongly influenced by the value attributed to disabled lives and whether or not they should even be born (Priestley 2003). Decisions of whether or not to give birth to a disabled baby are based on stereotypes of impairment and the perception that disabled lives equate to wrongful lives. That is, birth decisions are not based on the actual life that someone with certain biological characteristics might live. Rather, these choices are based on current knowledge of people with similar characteristics and how they live in the world today, and the low value put on disabled lives. Further advances in medical technology have increased the opportunities for society to find out about the biological characteristics of a child before birth. Indeed, this has increased the debate about whether or not they have the right to life. In this respect then, advances in technology have served to constrain the choices of disabled people from the beginning of their life-cycles. However, technology can be argued to be just a tool. The choice for technology to be used in this way is culturally embedded in discourses of personhood and citizenship that influence which human characteristics are socially acceptable and which are not; thus who should be born and who should not (Buchanan et al. 2000; Wolbring 2001).

As mentioned above, the life chances of individuals from different sub-groups are determined by different societal structures that create or block opportunities for them to participate in mainstream life. In the 1960s, the dominant view of an individual with an impairment was that their life was a personal tragedy. The focus was on the individual impairment and functional limitations, so the fact that disabled people were victims of inequalities and exclusion was legitimized as the result of deviating from the societal norm. Even today, with increasing awareness of the social model of disability, this conception still influences the life opportunities of disabled people and puts them at a significant disadvantage in terms of education and employment, thus limiting their horizons for action. It is more likely that the trajectories of young disabled people are scattered with obstacles and discrimination, thus putting them at a substantial disadvantage in relation to their non-disabled peers (Lewis, Robertson and Parsons 2005).

Quantitative evidence of the kind and degree of disadvantage encountered was explored in Chapter 2. In this study, the young disabled people's experiences of the special and mainstream education system and institutional culture of the schools, in part, reflected the differences in their aspirations. Young disabled people from mainstream schools were less likely than those from special schools to have aspirations to work in health and social care, although the opposite was the case for the career categories of education and sport. No young people based in special education had considered following education or sport-related careers, whereas girls and boys in mainstream schools aspired to become some kind of educational professional, including PE teacher, nursery teacher, disability equality trainer or language interpreter.

Further, boys from mainstream schools had an interest in sport, expressing a desire to pursue it as a career. The boys interested in sport went to a mainstream school with a strong focus on making sports inclusive for disabled people, and offered sports clubs to disabled students after school as well as classes as part of the curriculum. Other schools had different foci and priorities. Although it has been suggested that special schools have a limited curriculum compared to mainstream schools (see, for instance, Barnes 1991), they are more likely to have the resources and expertise to support and improve young disabled people's physical development and future health and independence. Thus young disabled people in special schools have regular exposure to health professionals, such as a physiotherapist, nurse and social worker. In contrast, mainstream schools are likely have a more academic focus, with the priority on exams and league tables.

Other factors that could impact on disabled people's life chances are family relationships and expectations (discussed further in Chapter 5). Parents are unlikely to have any premeditated aspirations for their disabled child compared to a non-disabled child (Shah 2005a) as a consequence of societal stereotypes of, and the low value attached to, disabled people. Parents are increasingly being given messages inferring that disabled lives equal wrongful lives and having a disabled baby is an expensive tragedy (Morris 1991). Therefore young disabled people have not been encouraged to have long-term aspirations because they were not expected to live to adulthood (Shah 2005a) and were not constructed as independent contributors to the social relations of production and reproduction (Priestley 2003). In western societies adults are defined by the extent to which they are self-supporting, self-reliant and autonomous in their functioning (Hockey and James 1993), and the fact that disabled people may need assistance to perform social or physical activities contributes to their presumed dependency, marginalization from adult status and exclusion from full adult rights and citizenship.

The young people in the current study all had aspirations to build independent futures for themselves, supporting themselves by getting a good job and contributing to the global economy. Although the primary focus of their stories was connected to education and employment, a few of the young people mentioned aspirations of living independently and having personal autonomy in adulthood, another important goal representing adult life. Most of these young people were based in special education and over the age of 16. Again this could be a consequence of the different foci of the special and mainstream education system. Zoë, aged 17, who wanted to work in childcare, also had plans to go to a further education college and to do an independence training course; as she says: 'I really want to live independently on my own, that's my aim.' Bob, aged 19, expressed the same aim and mentioned plans to go to the same college as Zoë after school to learn about how to live independently and break down perceptions, held by significant adults, that he will continue to depend on his parents for the rest of his life. Tim was the only respondent in the sample from mainstream school and under age 16 who mentioned independent living as a goal: '... basically I would um learn how to run my own house, I can't do that at the moment'; although he was not absolutely sure: 'but, um, I'd rather be living near my mum and dad'.

Conclusion

Social structures have a great influence on how young disabled people make choices, and indeed if and how they are met. This chapter analyses how structures in society, such as school, labour market and family, facilitate and constrain educational and career-related choices for marginalized groups. However, it also demonstrates the impact of personal factors on individual choice, including life history, age, gender, interests, social class and family background, which provide a range of options within their horizons for action. Further, young disabled people's own abilities and self-efficacy beliefs play a part in the construction and pursuit of their aspired goals. Individuals with strong self-efficacy beliefs, usually generated through repeated positive feedback of their actions, can combat barriers imposed by social structures by developing protective mechanisms of choice and change.

This chapter presents the perceptions and interactions of 33 young disabled people, based in special and mainstream schools, who are making choices about their future selves. They define how the game of choice is played in practice, and the players that determine the trajectory between the young person's original aspiration and actual destination. The chapter emphasizes the importance of listening to young disabled people whose voices have been muffled and choices have been constrained by disabling barriers and adult interpretations. This is crucial for ensuring that inequalities are not perpetuated and that young disabled people's future selves are products of their own choices.

Chapter 4

Choices and Opportunities in Mainstream and Special Education

Education is an important determinant for vocational choice. Schools are an introduction into the adult world, preparing young people for their future lives, particularly equipping them for the world of work. Thus, there are significant connections between the education and employment markets. This chapter explores the opportunity structures that operate within educational institutions that shape young disabled people's choices and contribute to their transitions. This stimulates the debate about individual choice, and how far it is determined by social structures (that is to say, school), systems and processes. It is followed by a discussion concerning the relationship between schools and work, and the ways institutional policy and practices, informal and formal, can make such connections stronger for some young people whilst weaker for others. Focusing on the debate concerning educational segregation and inclusion of disabled children/young people, this work presents young disabled people's perceptions of how their educational environment influences their choices and aspirations. It particularly notes the differences between mainstream and special education, focusing on the young people's experiences and views of three broad issues: learning opportunities (including post-school and career-related experiences) support, facilities and extra-curricular activities and friendships and social relationships. The chapter discusses current policy and practices in relation to the education of disabled people in Britain, drawing on debates propelled by Warnock. With the perspectives of young people, it attempts to identify change needed to facilitate inclusion in the future.

Introduction

Education is widely recognized to have an important role in the social, academic and economic progression of individuals and society. Education is increasingly perceived as responsible for teaching young people the skills necessary for them to engage in their communities and effectively participate in civic society, including the global labour market. One aim of education in today's global economy is to create an efficient and flexible workforce. As Tuckett (1997) argues, societies with adaptable and skilled labour are at a substantial economic advantage in relation to competitors in the global labour market.

In the modern world, with its transnational social connections and diverse customer base, it seems particularly important to provide all young people, disabled and non-disabled, with opportunities to contribute to the welfare of the economy. This is also central to the inclusion agenda of current UK government policy that is driven by the reality that excluding large groups of people from education, employment or any form of active engagement in society carries with it significant economic and social costs (DRC 2006). Recent trends have shown that there are a disproportionate number of young disabled people out of education, training and employment (Labour Force Survey 2005). Taking a social model perspective, this chapter explores how social structures in the education system limit disabled people's opportunities to achieve full citizenship. It integrates theory with empirical evidence to discuss how the social structures of school, mainstream and special, develop or restrain skills and talents that would facilitate young disabled people in producing increased social and economic gains in adulthood. The chapter assesses how, according to young disabled people, school practices and policies influence their formal learning opportunities, quality of support received, and friendships and social relationships.

There is general agreement that the experiences of disabled children in the UK have changed rapidly as a direct result of social transformation in the past two decades (Centre for Studies in Inclusive Education 2002; Priestley 2003). Policy developments such as the Disability Discrimination Act (1995; 2005), Special Educational Needs Disability Act (2001) and the Disability Equality Duty (2006) have led to more young disabled people being educated in mainstream schools than in the past. Further, more young disabled people are moving into further and higher education, and sitting public examinations (Davis and Watson 2001). According to the Audit Commission (2002), in 2001, 61 per cent of young disabled people in England were educated in mainstream schools, and only 4 per cent were not entered for any General Certificate of Secondary Education (GCSE) or General National Vocational Qualification (GNVQ) examinations. In special schools, 61 per cent of young people were not entered for examinations (Audit Commission 2002), thus indicating the significance of school type for the educational opportunities of disabled people.

Barnes (1991) has argued that inclusion is imperative in the fight for the elimination of discrimination and for disabled people being accepted as full citizens by the social majority. Co-operative learning can promote greater interpersonal attractions and more positive interactions between disabled and non-disabled peers, with social benefits extending beyond the classroom and becoming long-term (Putnam 1993). This is endorsed by Meyer (2001), who finds that mainstream schooling increases the mixture and quality of friendship groups of young disabled people.

Being educated in an inclusive environment is positively correlated with the successful transition of individuals with disabilities into employment and wider society (Jenkinson 1997; Shah, Travers and Arnold 2004a). Further, inclusive education can (for some people) facilitate the establishment of social relationships between disabled and non-disabled peers, as awareness and understanding of disability is said to engender an increasing acceptance of it (Shah 2005a; Wertheimer 1997). Moreover, it presents disabled people with an equal training to their non-disabled counterparts and, therefore, qualifications to compete with them in mainstream economic society.

However, the integration and inclusion of disabled children is far from complete and the process has encountered many barriers that have influenced the aspirations and opportunities of young disabled people. A report by Abrams (2004, 18), headlined *Inclusion is Just an Illusion* states that while schools are 'talking the talk', they are still not 'walking the walk'. Ofsted (2004) finds that while there was a growing awareness of the need to treat all pupils equally, there was still a mismatch between schools' aspirations and reality. This has been echoed by Macbeath et al. (2006) in their recent report, *The Cost of Inclusion.* They argue that mainstream schools often could not provide the facilities and expertise required for teaching some young disabled people. This inevitably led to young people's exclusion within the school and put a strain on their parents and teachers.

Baroness Warnock, a former advocate of inclusion, concurs that inclusion has gone too far because it has resulted in the closure of special schools, to the detriment of disabled children. She recently called for a radical review of education for disabled children, perceiving the solution to be to return to the special education institutions of the past, so that disabled children could receive specialist support and teaching. However, this is not necessarily the best way forward as special schools have a number of shortcomings for disabled children including, as Davis and Watson (2001, 671) argue, 'being locked away in isolated residential settings'.

Structural forces impinge on both mainstream and special schools, and teachers either facilitate or restrict young disabled people's aspirations in a number of ways. However, whilst much current debate focuses on variation in the extent to which young disabled people in mainstream schools are fully included, there is little research that compares the aspirations of those in mainstream and special schools. This chapter explores if and how special and mainstream schools affect young disabled people's aspirations for future education and employment. Using qualitative data from a number of young disabled people in special and mainstream schools, the chapter illustrates how young disabled people's encounters with different structures serve to reinforce their difference or 'normality' within the schools. It also highlights the views of educationalists about similar issues. As in the preceding chapters, disabled young people are presented as critical social actors who are telling their own stories of how they perceive school has shaped their choices and aspirations for their future selves.

Learning Opportunities

School frames the choices of young people via a number of practices, in addition to the core curriculum. Several factors, embedded in the social structure of schools, are equally if not more important to young people's future selves. These include relationships with teachers, teachers' expectations of young disabled people, peer relationships in and out of the classroom, support available, the extent to which young people engage with the subjects taught and the institutional foci of the school. Often it is an interplay of these experiences that make more of an impression on young people's prospective choices, and their vision of society as a whole, rather than stand-alone 'core' subjects of the formal curriculum, argued as being a prescribed and regimented duty young people have no choice but to submit to (Cullingford 2002). This is not to say that core subjects in school do not influence young people's future employment, but that they do so in combination with discussions with others, dynamics of the classroom, social relationships with class peers and teachers, the social composition of the school, and single events and turning points.

Despite the government's drive via recent UK government legislation (including the Special Educational Needs and Disability Act (2001) or Part 4 of the Disability Discrimination Act (1995) and DDA (2005)) to encourage all members of society to work together to create and realize desirable and inclusive futures, disabled children have not been given the same educational opportunities as their nondisabled peers. In the regime of the 'education market' (Ball, Bowe and Gerwitz 1994) schools try to attract the ablest pupils because they are perceived to contribute the most to the wealth of the nation and success of school league tables. Disabled children/young people are excluded as they are not regarded as future economically contributing citizens, and expectations that they will progress up career ladders are rare (Middleton 2003). This perspective gives schools less of an incentive to spend time and resources creating an inclusive environment to ensure that young disabled people, who are perceived to be disruptive and harmful to the school's success in achieving specific targets (Barnes 1991; Lloyd-Smith and Tarr 2000), have equal opportunities to non-disabled peers.

Formal and informal structures of the classroom provide young people with positive and negative experiences that open up and narrow down future choices. For instance, schools provide information about the gender distribution of careers within the labour market and the level of qualifications typically required for each (Furlong and Biggart 1999). Further, schools are expected to instil young people with the experience of social values and behaviour, at the same time as developing the skills, habits and abilities (for example, discipline, punctuality, initiative) from which they can make choices relevant to the world of work. As Foskett and Hemsley-Brown (2001) argue, decisions about following certain trajectories are not always a product of positive experiences but could be a response to failure. Young disabled people in the current study mentioned several encounters with disabling barriers that caused them to be differentially constructed, and excluded from learning opportunities in the classroom, thus restricting occupational possibilities. For example, Mike had to force other students to work with him when they did group work at school: 'people don't actually come to me and say "oh I'll work with you", but I'm in my class I'm actually like excluded when people are grouped and stuff'. This supports writers including Halsey et al (1997) and Vickerstaff (2003) who contend that many aspects of schooling reinforce social divisions and marginalization. Further, access to education and rates of success are highly correlated with gender, class and disability.

Post-School Choices

Negative and positive experiences in classrooms also influenced young people's decisions of whether or not to pursue a particular subject further, thus narrowing options for subsequent employment. For instance, Tommo, who wanted to be a sports assistant, went to a mainstream school with a particular focus on sports for disabled and non-disabled young people. He was very enthusiastic about his sports lessons, during and after school, perceiving his classes and the sports facilities for disabled students to be the best things about school:

> They've got like good facilities and that, for like all different people some of the sports they do like rugby and that, those that can't do it do other sports that are like in the, in the national curriculum, like Boccia and golf ball. When you play it you have to have a blind-fold on and the ball gets pushed to you. So you know the direction that it's going, it's got a bell inside it.

> My best one's PE I can tell you that … No one can take me out my PE lessons says me and that's the bottom line … I'm hoping for an excellent grade at the end of year 11 … I'm going to do that as well, I'm gonna go to college … then hopefully I'll go through to uni to do the same thing in order to qualify to work as a sports assistant.

Ikky's post-school choices were influenced, to an extent, by his Information Technology class, which he enjoyed at school and wanted to continue at college. He perceived this would lead to a good job: 'IT is my main subject and I'm gonna get a job with IT … like design software or like put programs on them, stuff like that.'

Sometimes school teachers have a significant influence on what young people choose to do in the future. The quality of relationship between the teacher and young person is likely to partly determine whether the young person enjoys the subject taught, is good at it, and is likely to take it forward to the next stage. Levels of encouragement by teachers could pay real dividends to students' confidence in pursuing certain trajectories (Furlong and Biggart 1999). Jussim and Eccles (1992) point out that when teachers expect more of their students, the students learn more; when teachers expect less, students learn less. Likewise, Steinberg (2002) contends that when students receive more attention from teachers, they are more likely to experience classes that are engaging and positively challenging. For example, Dan, who wanted to be a carpenter after school, was definitely not a great school enthusiast and on the whole believed school would be more enjoyable 'by getting rid of the staff and letting the kids run the school'. However, he enjoyed art at school and identified his art teacher as significant to his post-school choice to study woodwork at college: 'the good things would be the lessons and my art teacher who gives me advice really'.

Tommo identified a few of his teachers as supportive of his ambition to be a sports assistant: 'I've told quite a few of my teachers ... they said I'd be able to make a good sports assistant.' Although Tommo did not mention which particular teachers were supportive, it can be assumed that one of them was his PE teacher as PE was his favourite subject and he believed he was good at it: 'I'm good at sports and the theory part of it where you learn all the muscles and the bones ...'

There are many ways in which school influences young people's subsequent choices for their future life. While it influences positive choices, as can be seen above, it can also influence negative decisions. Foskett and Hemsley-Brown (2001) suggest that new choices are made in the aftermath of a failure to achieve some other learning ambition. For example, Tommo's unwillingness or inability to be 'one of the crowd' in mainstream school could have ignited negative peer relationships that influenced his perception of drama class, and thus his choices not to pursue drama to the next level: 'I'm not that keen on drama any more 'cos half the people in there they mess about they don't hardly do the work.'

On a similar note, Ikky developed negative impressions about maths after his classroom experiences: 'I don't like the class, there's too much noise and messing about', and this also influenced his post-school decision not to include maths. Although it was not explicit from their narrative, it is not unreasonable to suggest that the boys' negativity towards their classes was influenced by the fact that they felt excluded from entering the informal classroom culture of their peers, which involved executing behaviour beyond their physical abilities. Thus it could be argued that this reinforced the disabled/non-disabled divide and contributed to their negative experiences in the classroom.

Like Tommo and Ikky, several of the young disabled people based in mainstream education in this study had considered post-school choices in connection with formal experiences of schooling and their career aspirations. Three young people, Mike, Sam and Sabrina, aged 15, 17 and 14 respectively, all went to the same mainstream school that focused on academic qualifications and encouraged young people to continue education beyond the age of 16. As the Special Educational Needs Co-ordinator put it: 'We'd like to think that all youngsters, if they want to, can carry on their education here right up to the age of 18. We do have numerous examples of disabled youngsters carrying on into post-16 education.'

It is likely that this expectation had an influence on the post-school choices of Mike, Sabrina and Sam, who all had clearly defined goals and had expressed a desire to continue their education to university level in areas which qualified them to meet their career aspirations:

> I'm gonna stay on until sixth form ... I would like to go to university um, maybe um, one in France 'cos my aunty went to university in France ... I want to be a language interpreter, French and Spanish. (Sabrina, aged 14)

> I've chosen [GCSE] French, IT, erm, English, science, maths, just the basic subjects because they're good for the career I want to do, then A Levels ... after that university. (Mike, aged 15)

> I do um psychology, business and media ... I've just had my AS exams ... I want to sort of go to university erm, I'm a bit undecided about what I want to do at the moment erm, I'll probably do something to do with either business or media like erm management or something like that or media production. (Sam, aged 17)

In general the young disabled people, based in mainstream school, who had clearly defined goals (see Chapter 3), tended to be clear about what they wanted to do after school. Their choices were similar to those for non-disabled young people who were part of the studies by Foskett and Hesketh (1996) and Foskett and Hemsley-Brown (2001). Their post-school plans involved going to college or university to follow a course connected to their career aspirations. This supports Vickerstaff (2003) who suggests that since the turn of the millennium more young people expect to continue education after compulsory school-leaving age, rather than going straight into paid work.

However, the young people with wide-ranging goals were undecided, but there were exceptions. For example, Tim had wide-ranging goals with regards to employment but had aspirations to live independently and have his own home. It was the latter that influenced the certainty of his post-school transitions: 'After year 11 I'm going to college X ... I definitely want to go to college, the reason is, is because, um, I need life skills and I've not got that at the moment. So, I need new life skills ... to learn to run my own home.'

A minority of young people who had wide-ranging choices had been considering post-school options. Millie, who mentioned a few goals within the performing arts field, had been thinking about her future, assessing her options and considering what might be required to meet her goals: 'it seems a long way off ... I'll see what I get in my grades and if it's not as good and it can't really get me a job I probably try and go up to university.' Similarly Nay, who expressed an interest in a range of occupations including music, sport and drama, had considered his post-school choices: 'I want to go to college to do either drama or media studies or computer studies.' Other young people with wide-ranging goals had not considered what they would do after school. Typical responses included silence or comments such as 'Not really thought about it'.

The structures of special schools influenced young disabled people's post-school opportunities in different ways. The empirical data suggests that the special schools considered support and access provision to be a priority of post-school transitions, before academic or career aspirations. Some educational professionals expressed concerns that young disabled people might not be able to meet any aspirations if strategies for suitable support and access to required education and training were not in place:

> ... considerations when deciding where students go after school are the facilities of the establishment, we look at facilities on offer, the courses and also access issues as well as the sort of support the student will require. A whole host of factors and issues are considered. We raise the issues with the establishment regarding the student. The colleges are told by us that students 'abc' could access their courses if they provide 'xyz' in addition. Gradually we, in this way, nibble away at the FE establishments themselves and at the local authority as we feel that now we are in a unitary authority there are less opportunities particularly for those with physical impairments. (Teacher in Special School)

The access and resource limitations of several mainstream secondary schools may mean that young disabled people have to move to designated schools, with suitable facilities for disabled people, several miles from their home while their local non-disabled peers can make a straight transition to their local secondary school (Pitt and Curtin 2004; Shah 2005b). This is not only tiring for young disabled people, as they need to travel long distances, but also means that they may be separated socially from friends made at school and peers from their home locality. Therefore this situation is not much different to being in a special school, except even designated mainstream schools fail in terms of access and support provision compared to specialist institutions. As Fiona pointed out:

> I had a few problems. I wanted to do beauty first, but er, I had a few problems with the [mainstream] college and that ... discrimination ... they kept just avoiding it, saying that I can't apply ... They didn't help a lot so, so I gradually began to like photography ...

I've been accepted by X [special] college to do photography. (Fiona, aged 18, special school)

The college I chose doesn't specialise in what I want to do [drama] but X college does. I went to look around ... the staff said, 'why didn't you like it?', because, I said 'I feel like I'm in a room full of people who don't give a peg what you think or feel' ... This college I have chosen, they know me because I was assessed over three days and not over one day. So I wasn't assessed for long enough at the college I turned down. (Tyson, aged 19, special school)

Other young people took it for granted that they would automatically follow the special education route from primary school to further education college like their friends who had already made that transition. This was particularly the case for the 13–16 year-olds, who had all been in special education since they were infants. They were still in contact with peers who had left school in previous years, and were keen to join them at the sixth form special school:

I'm going to school B [special] for two or three years, 'cos my mates are gonna be there ... then college X [special] ... It's easier to go through the system ... Lots of people do it this way. (Quentin, aged 15, special school)

Leaving school next year ... [going to] B school because all my friends have gone there. (Cathy, aged 14, special school)

Going to go to B school, that's like errm, a special like school thing. It's like, it's like here, but it's, like, got a sixth form in it ... 'cos my mates are, it's 'cos my mates used to go from here, you see. (Quentin, aged 15, special school)

As mentioned previously, support and access were important considerations for young people in special schools when making an institutional choice. Experiences of partial integration in local mainstream schools seemed to shape young people's transitional choices. For instance, Cathy was partially integrated into her local comprehensive school for a term, on a two days a week basis. However, she was placed in a Pupil Referral Unit and thus segregated within a mainstream school. It was the experience of being segregated and unsupported that influenced her choice to continue her education beyond 16 in a special education institution:

They didn't know my disability. I felt as though I was shoved out and not with other people, you know ... they've got this special unit and I was in there quite a bit. I wanted to be in the mainstream school bit but I was in there, I just thought it was useless ... because I made friends but I didn't get chance to talk to them ... I told them that I don't want to go again no.

On a similar note, Zoë, who had spent some time at mainstream comprehensive as part of a link placement organized by her special school, found non-disabled peers difficult to handle and thus had no real desire to go to a mainstream college after being in the supportive environment of a special school for 15 years: 'pupils was horrible, well they weren't horrible but when you asked them to move they used to give you such funny looks and things like that ... At mainstream school I think they would not support as much.'

Even where young people had not experienced mainstream education themselves, some had a prejudice towards it, based on the views and experiences of peers. For instance, although Rob and Quentin had never been to a mainstream school, their classmates Cathy and Noalga had shared experiences with them that influenced their perceptions of mainstream schools and their choice not to include mainstream education in their post-school options. In response to the question 'have you considered going to mainstream school after here?' Quentin answered: 'No I just, I couldn't get on with mainstream ... there's people that like mainstream and people that don't and I'm one of those people that don't like mainstream ... [Cathy] has been ... the staff weren't umm brilliant when she went so she's here full time now.' From Rob's interview it became clear that he feared going to mainstream school 'in case you get all picked on and stuff'.

While mainstream education hindered young people's trajectories as a result of its exclusionary practices and procedures that reinforced their differences, special education also served to do so in different ways. Research by Dr John Mary and the British Council Of Disabled People (BCODP) (1986) shows that the special education system is one of the main channels for disseminating able-bodied minded perceptions of the world and ensuring that disabled school leavers are socially isolated. This isolation results in disabled people passively accepting social discrimination, lacking the skills necessary to pursue the tasks of adulthood successfully, and not understanding the main social issues of our time. As well as reinforcing the myth that disabled people are 'eternal children', segregated education ensures disabled school leavers lack the skills for overcoming this myth (BCODP 1986). Jenkinson (1997) and Fuchs and Fuchs (1998) support this research, arguing that lack of appropriate behavioural role models, lack of feedback from non-disabled peers and removal from the common culture of childhood and adolescence contribute to special school students' later isolation in the community.

A further major criticism of special schools is that their isolated curricula focus disproportionately on specific educational needs, preventing students from learning the wide range of subjects offered in mainstream school that are important for successful economic participation. Jenkinson (1997) also suggests that the small number of staff in special schools, coupled with their significantly limited, if not deficient, curricula expertise, serves to restrict the range and content of the curriculum and so young disabled people's opportunities to meet career aspirations.

Some of the young people in this study who were based in mainstream schools viewed special schools more like hospitals than schools, with resources and expertise more concerned with supporting young disabled people's physical development, future health and independence rather than providing academic opportunities on a par with non-disabled peers. These young people felt that peers in special schools were different from them. Although they recognized the problems of mainstream schools they felt that special schools would isolate them from their non-disabled peers, and restrict the academic and social opportunities they needed to achieve a successful adulthood in the 'real' world:

> I've seen special schools but I don't really like them 'cos I don't really like seeing all the people 'cos like, they can't talk ... I don't think they do languages at special school. (Sabrina, aged 14)

> I've never ... I've looked around them [special schools] but I've never actually gone ... No I don't think it would be the same because I want it to be a mixture of people not just people in chairs like me ... I'd feel quite quiet 'cos I wouldn't be able to say my feelings because people might be worse off than me. (Millie, aged 13)

> I got my laptop from the special school, I had to go there to see it, but I just saw all these like really ill people, you know like in beds and stuff, I don't think I could handle that. (Mike, aged 15)

> They [children at special school] can't like move like that good, and there's quite a few at X special school. Special schools have kids who are more disabled than those at mainstream. (Tommo, aged 15)

Some young people based in special educational institutions expressed disappointment about the curriculum and the expectations in special schools. They considered the level of work to be lower than their level of ability:

> They didn't seem to push you. Like we didn't do A Levels or anything ... I would have liked to have a chance at some proper tests and see how far I got, see how clever I was you know ... they don't seem to push you at special school. (Schumacher, aged 20)

> Music and communications, I don't like them ... communications we hardly do anything in the lesson, and music is just like playing music and you don't, you don't learn anything from that. (Paul, aged 20)

> The staff are nice, but it's the lessons I can't cope sometimes ... just too slow, should be a little faster. (Rob, aged 16)

So the opportunity structures of mainstream and special education systems, as they currently stand, both play a part in shaping the post-school options of young disabled people. However, the limitations of both systems, as described above, mean that young disabled people have to make sacrifices. As Hodkinson, Sparkes and Hodkinson (1996) contend, young people's horizons for action are limited to what is available within that segment of the education market. The Cabinet Office report (2005) confirms that there is a range of disabling barriers that can cause disruption to the education of young disabled people, restrict their learning opportunities and delay their progression to adulthood. The post-school choices of young disabled people may be counter to what others think could and should be achieved by someone with their impairment (Adams and Holland 2006). As a DRC (2003) study finds, three in ten young disabled people had not gone into higher or further education for reasons relating to their impairment. As long as this continues, the future selves of young disabled people become less of a reflection of their own choices and aspirations, and more a result of the disabling structures in education and society.

Work Experience

A valuable part of school/college life that has an influence on a young person's occupational choices, directly or indirectly, is a period of work experience. Work experience placements offer many benefits and learning opportunities. Broad objectives in the policy statement include employability skills, personal and social development. Further, it has been suggested by the National Council for Work Experience that work experience is important for building confidence, consolidating skills and helping young people to progress to employment. Their research found that 44 per cent of students and graduates considered work experience an important factor in making decisions about their occupational futures.

Guile and Griffiths (2001) contend that new EU policy has indicated a need to reassess the relationships between education and work based on the expanding global market. They argue that new curriculum frameworks are required to support students which relate 'vertical development' (intellectual development generated through formal schooling) to 'horizontal development' (changes and development of identity and skills that occur through movement between different contexts, such as the workplace, the school or the community centre). These frameworks should encourage students to make links between work experience, its underlying knowledge and skill, and its context.

Therefore, work experience in school and college is essential for developing young people's understandings about changes in the 'world of work', to enhance their key skills and to make closer links between their formal programmes of study and the world of work (Green, Leney and Wolf 1999). Fischer and Stuber (1998) argue that a combination of theoretical and practical learning prepares young people to engage more rapidly with new employment requirements and enables them to move into alternative work environments more easily. It can promote an understanding about different types of employment and the extent to which the work environment reflects the young disabled people's interests, knowledge, personality and ability. This was considered important by both young people and educational professionals in special schools:

> Work experience will be very good because I don't know what I can do and what I can't do, in a situation of work. (Zoë, aged 17)

> Sometimes you have to take the student to a particular work situation because they may not be aware of what the job entails. They need the hands-on opportunity. (Teacher)

The young disabled people in this study thought work experience was a good idea to give them an understanding of what activities they are best capable of performing, and the extent to which these activities will best satisfy their survival, pleasure and contribution needs. Therefore through this process the young person can explore career options, see what work life is really like, and get certain experiences that directly influence their career choice and work behaviour. Further it gives young people an opportunity to learn about what they like and dislike about the type of employment in which they are engaged (Ferry 2003). This was echoed by one of the young disabled people based in special school: 'I might be going for a job at Theatre Royal ... Like doing a proper job, like doing the tickets on the door and ... I went for work experience and the boss, the boss wanted somebody and I said I'd put my name down for the job' (Rob, aged 16).

However, the young disabled people from a sixth form special school had never been on a work experience placement, even during their secondary education, which was at the same institution. They all had clearly defined goals for their future lives and considered that a work experience placement would have been beneficial to the attainment of work-based skills, knowledge of what the world of work is like and how it differs from being taught about employment in school:

> No I haven't [done work experience] but I would like to ... I definitely think it would be helpful well, because I've nearly left school they [teachers] don't see any point, I'll probably do it when I get to college. Probably. (Hannah, aged 18)

> A friend of mine from here's on work experience today. I'd like to do some of that. (Tyson, aged 19)

The educational professionals of this special school concurred with the young people, considering that work experience would be beneficial to the young people in terms of helping them to determine what are realistic and unrealistic goals for them to pursue. However, they believed that work placements should match the young people's career aspirations in order to be truly valuable: 'What we hope to do is avoid placing people on a placement outside of school that doesn't meet their careers aspirations and isn't a work placement for the sake of work placement.'

According to the Cabinet Office report (2005), young disabled people's opportunities to do work experience may be hindered by child protection and health and safety legislation, which promotes a risk-averse culture amongst employers. Work experience is not covered by Access to Work or the Disability Discrimination Act in the same way as full-time employment. This means that funds are not available for support or extra equipment required by the young person while on the placement. It was the lack of support provision that prevented the young disabled people from the sixth form special school, who had high-level support needs, from having opportunities to do work experience. As their deputy head teacher pointed out:

> Whilst it is almost easy to find people to provide work placement, while it is easy to find places that are accessible in terms of the physical environment, in terms of providing any care needs that the individual may require during the day – it is very difficult ... In the past, when the school had a lot of staffing, we used to be able to ring up people to go out and we used to be able to use residential staff, extra staff to support that. At the moment we haven't got that staffing capacity.

However, the other special school involved in the study managed to overcome support-related barriers so young people had the opportunities to do some work experience. Unlike the specialist sixth form school, it operated a policy that was more focused on providing students with the experience of work rather than meeting individual aspirations. The placements offered were based on a professional partnership between the school and the workplace that had been in place for a period of time. This partnership ensured that the workplace was accessible and that the young people had the support they required while on placement. So although the placements were not directly connected with the young people's career aspirations, accessibility and support were guaranteed so the young people could go and take part:

> The partnership between school and workplace is very strong, we used to have a greater number of workplaces but now it is more difficult as health and safety regulations have made it more difficult to place students ... We have a good relationship with the X centre as a venue for work experience. It provides a wide range of possibilities to look at the experience of work as opposed to jobs ... The purpose of work experience in this setting is to increase their confidence and to bring them to experience being in a different kind of setting. It has a broader undertone to it than a work experience might. (Teacher at special school)

The students interviewed from this specialist secondary school all expected to go to the same venue for work experience placement, like their friends had done in previous years, regardless of their individual career aspirations. For example, Rob had already been on work placement and Cathy and Quentin expected to go to the same place for their work experience:

> I went for work experience at the theatre in the city... I went to the ticket office, met the people in the ticket office and errm I went to the call centre. (Rob, aged 16)

> I'm doing that next year, before I leave school ... I might go to where Rob went, the concert hall in X [city]. (Cathy, aged 14)

> I'll do that [work experience] next year ... Rob did it before half term ... Yep he told me what it was like. (Quentin, aged 15)

Noalga, whose ambition was to study multimedia at college after school and ultimately follow a path in that area, communicated that he would do work experience 'next year ... At theatre'. When asked, he confirmed that it was the same work placement as his peers Rob and Wendy.

However, it can be argued that this is an example of how social structures of special school and workplaces can limit young disabled people's learning opportunities and thus their horizons for action in their adult lives. Further, they determine the nature of citizenship, which, from an individualist perspective, emerges from the choices agents make (Pattie, Seyd and Whiteley 2004). So, while this special school gave young people opportunities to be involved in a work placement, it did not promote their self-determination to exercise their choices and contribute to decisions about what kind of placement it should be. Rather, it reinforced a medical model approach, where young disabled people are passive recipients of adult choices, and the focus is on changing the disabled individual, not the disabling environment. As Duffy (2003, 5) puts it, 'if you have self-determination then this means you are in charge of your own life. If you do not have self-determination then other people are in charge of you.' As long as special schools fail to incorporate the social model of disability into debates on citizenship, disabled people will continue to be disadvantaged through their life course. Barnes, Mercer and Shakespeare (2003, 104) endorse this; they describe the special education system as 'a key element in the creation and perpetuation of the social oppression of disabled people.'

While some parents, professionals and young disabled people claim special education is worthwhile (Barnes, Mercer and Shakespeare 2003; Jenkinson 1998), the evidence suggests that aspects of the special education system, including its social structures and regulatory policies, are failing to promote young disabled people's autonomy and self-determination, and thus their rights to full citizenship. Preventing young disabled people from exercising their civil rights, denying them opportunities to participate in community decision-making and ignoring their contribution in relation to school work experience can lead to subsequent

Library
Knowledge Spa
Royal Cornwall Hospital
Treliske
Truro. TR1 3HD

inequalities or exclusion from social and economic adult communities. This was highlighted in the Russell Commission's consultation document in 2005. It identifies the need to consider young disabled people when developing policies to encourage active citizenship. The consultation document recognizes young disabled people as being 'one of a number of groups on whom particular attention needs to be focussed in order to increase their levels of participation' particularly in relation to work experience (Russell Commission 2005, 24).

The empirical evidence from this study suggests that young disabled people based in mainstream schools had very different experiences in relation to work experience. They expected their work placement, like their post-school transitions, to be connected to their career aspirations, not their support and access needs. However, work experience programmes varied in each of the four mainstream schools involved in the study. One school encouraged their students to take primary responsibility in selecting and organizing the placement. According to the school's Special Educational Needs Co-ordinator and the Deputy Head Teacher: 'there is the expectation that all our year 10 students find their own placements but we will help them, if they are having any difficulty or trouble ... They make decisions but we guide them ... I've never known anyone not go to where they didn't want to be.'

Both Mike and Sabrina, from that mainstream school, had clearly defined post-school goals, in terms of possible career paths, and were keen to choose a work placement related to their own goals. Mike, who wanted to be a journalist or a fiction author, had done some work experience before: 'I did work experience in May um I did it at the town library because I said I'm a big reader and um, in year 7 I was a library monitor so I did the books and stuff there. I've always wanted to help with that as well.'

Sabrina expected to do a placement the following year in relation to her aspiration to be a language interpreter: 'I want to um work in an interpreting centre.'

However, although the young people were encouraged to make their own choices, they felt these were not always supported by school policies and practices:

> The work experience? There's a teacher, Mrs [W] special needs she sorts it out the placement and the transport and stuff and then that's it I just do all the work, get there, but when I went that time school couldn't organize transport, and it was a 40-minute walk from my house so my dad had to take me and my mum picked me up, so because there wasn't any transport, proper one [with wheelchair access], we had to walk it, back and forth. (Mike, aged 15)

In the above instance Mike's own resilience and family support network overcame the barriers created by the school. However, without this he would have been prevented from being involved in activities that could have a significant impact on future employment and lifestyle opportunities. Although structures of this mainstream school encouraged self-determination, they still denied young disabled people's full citizenship by restricting their participation and contribution to learning opportunities that were fully accessible to non-disabled peers.

Other mainstream schools involved in the study operated work experience programmes based on partnerships between the school and the workplace, ensuring support and access were in place:

> We've got a work experience co-ordinator. She works with the SENCO to ensure that youngsters with physical disabilities are given an appropriate placement. (Deputy Head Teacher)

> We have good contacts with employers, particularly with good employers of those with disabilities and we work hard to ensure they do get work experience. That might entail our TAs transporting them to and from work, or in some cases actually being there on work experience albeit as much in the background as possible. It depends on the disability. (Special Educational Needs Co-ordinator)

Unlike the secondary special school, the mainstream schools had established partnerships with several workplaces so placements could be connected to young people's own choices and aspirations:

> It's their choice. Definitely. Checka wanted to go to Connexions ... she went. We did actually get some really good placements but again, long-term planning, we've been speaking to people about Nay since year 10 and we're getting him a two-week placement at the concert hall in the city because that's what he wants to do. (Assistant Special Educational Needs Co-ordinator)

> It is fairly difficult to find employers to give disabled students placements. It depends on what the students want. The district council are very good. P College is very good and B special school, so if they want a school environment, special or mainstream, we can provide it. So far we have always found what they have wanted: IT at P [college], medical placements at the hospital. We work with students ... it doesn't always fit in with their aspirations. This last year a student wanted to go somewhere but they couldn't take him, couldn't or wouldn't, so we looked at something else. That happens to a lot of students. (Special Educational Needs Coordinator)

One of the partnerships was with the secondary special school as it met with the health and safety requirements and offered a supportive accessible environment. However, the placement also provided the young people with opportunities to work in areas related to their individual aspirations. For example, Tommo and Dan, the aspiring carpenter and sports assistant, expected to go to the same special school for their work placement, although wanted to experience different fields of work:

> I want something with sports ... I would do it here or at X [special school] ... Teaching the children sports. (Tommo, aged 15)

> They're still trying to find me a place ... actually working in a school helping people with a disability, like teaching woodwork, helping them do stuff. (Dan, aged 15)

Even where schools had several links with employers, the fact that work experience was not covered by the Disability Discrimination Act or Access to Work did place restrictions on disabled students' learning opportunities. For example, Steve, whose post-school choices involved going to university to study English with a view to become a freelance writer, felt that his work placement was more focused on accommodating his access needs than career ambitions: 'I've had three weeks work experience while I've been here ... two weeks at a special college doing various bits err and bobs there, but mainly to do with building my computer skills more than, more than to do with future career I think' (Steve, aged 17).

The Russell Commission (2005) has recognized this as a serious barrier to young disabled people's full citizenship in mainstream society. As a consequence, recommendations have been made that the government review the case for making funding available to provide reasonable adjustments for work experience placements, in the same way that the Department for Work and Pensions (DWP) makes funding available for reasonable adjustments for employees through the Access to Work programme (Joint Committee on the Draft Disability Discrimination Bill 2004, 95).

Support and Facilities

Despite the government's policy drive towards inclusion, this chapter suggests that without the participative involvement of disabled people, full inclusion cannot be achieved. Further it highlights the views of young disabled people who have had positive experiences in special school, but been oppressed by their social structures and underrepresented in literature and policy, more concerned with the negative aspects of special schooling (Gray 2002). For instance, several young people, based in special school, had experienced both types of education system but praised the support and facilities in special education institutions. They felt these were not available in mainstream school on the same scale. Facilities including physiotherapy, speech therapy and accessible swimming/hydrotherapy pools were perceived to be crucial to some young people for their physical development, future health and independence, and thus successful adulthood:

> The two really good things about this school are swimming and physio ... I think it's very important for me to get out of the chair and have a good stretch. (Cathy, aged 14)

> When I came here I only looked like a newborn baby, 'cos I was so small ... The school has really helped me grow into an adult. (Zoë, aged 17)

Tyson, a young woman of 19, who had been at the same school since the age of three, was a strong advocate for special schools. She was firmly opposed to the government's decision to close them down. Like Warnock (2005), she considered special schools to be vital for the physical and social survival of young disabled people like herself:

> The government just ain't got a clue, 'cos they think 'Oh the special schools will be out in a minute' but, but when you see pupils like some of the ones here, they wouldn't be alive if they didn't have special school.

Here, Tyson was not only referring to the physically accessible environment of special schools, but also the strong sense of support, social acceptance and inclusion it permitted. She felt this was not available in mainstream schools, recalling her experiences of being partially integrated into the local mainstream comprehensive:

> They [non-disabled young people] kept setting the fire alarm off, lovely and that was all 'cos they knew we were in on that day ... there was no classroom space, and you had to queue ages for the bathroom because there was only X amount of accessible toilets ...The link with X school was a good idea in theory, but the last two years there didn't really work and we fought not to go from year two.

This was also the case for her classmate Zoë who, as is shown earlier in the chapter, felt socially disabled in mainstream school.

These voices echo those of some of the disabled students in studies by Pitt and Curtin (2004) and Cook, Swain and French (2001), who were also positive about special education and the opportunities it offered. The young disabled people in the present study felt special school offered them a better quality of life, with opportunities and support to develop personally and socially. They believed their development would be hindered by mainstream education with its lack of appropriate resources and provision: 'At mainstream school I think they would not support as much they would probably say you're not able to' (Zoë, aged 17).

Lack of adequate resources and support prevented some of the disabled students in mainstream schools from engaging in certain activities. However, some took up the opportunity to use the therapeutic and sports facilities of special schools that were more accessible to them:

> My physio is based at X special school, I go swimming there every other week. (Allan, aged 13)

> There is a special school not far from here, school X, they've got their own hydrotherapy pool ... It's for these kids who can't like go in cold baths, cold swimming baths. We use their pool, they let us use their pool. (Tommo, aged 15)

I used to go to X [special school] to swim when I was 8–10 year ... I don't go swimming at this school. (Ikky, aged 15)

Some of the young people thought lack of support was a significant problem at mainstream schools. They felt it restricted them from pursuing their own aspirations, and did not really give them a choice to participate in and contribute to formal and informal learning. As Hannah put it:

I lived in Africa, it was [mainstream school], they just couldn't cope with me they, they just didn't have the facilities that they've got in a special school ... my mum taught me to read and write at home ... Here [in special school] I'm supported to do what I want.

This is supported by Martin (2004) who has suggested that young disabled people feel they receive insufficient support in school and are discouraged from taking standard educational qualifications required for university entrance. Further, as explored above, they are often prevented from studying subjects of their choice due to poor access to the curriculum and the disabling environment of mainstream schools and college (Burgess 2003).

Educational Support and Teaching Assistants

Another resource employed to facilitate the educational opportunities of young disabled people is the appointment of teaching assistants (TA), primarily to support disabled students in mainstream schools. Their roles are varied and include advising class teachers on issues such as adapting teaching styles and classroom organization to cater for the diversity of children, developing an accessible curriculum and monitoring individual programmes where necessary (Shaw 1998). Teaching assistants also work with individual young people on specific learning tasks. However, Ofsted (2004) reports that one of the weaknesses of inclusion preventing disabled students reaching their full potential is the use and quality of teaching assistants. A recent Ofsted (2006) study, *Inclusion: Does it Matter Where Pupils Are Taught?* finds that young disabled people were less likely to make good academic progress in mainstream schools where teaching assistants were the main means of support. Similarly, Priestley (1998) found that for some young disabled people, the physical proximity of the helper could work against social processes of acceptance among other children in the class. This can also be illustrated by the current work: 'I don't like having a TA around me all the time because I want some of my own space ... it's not really fair on my friends having to sit next to a TA all the time when I want to sit with them' (Millie, aged 13).

Allan (1996, 222) suggests that all aspects of the child's interpersonal relationships can be brought under the vigilance of the staff, as disabled children are more comprehensively observed than their non-disabled peers. This promotes a divide between young disabled people and their non-disabled peers. For example, Checka, aged 15, felt that the adult support she received restricted her from engaging in normal activities with friends outside the classroom. This again can be seen to hinder the formation of friendships and social networks, and reinforce the powerful messages that disabled people are different and need 'looking after':

> I'm not allowed in the playground, I'm sitting in the classroom with the TAs, all day 'cause they think I'd run away.

> No, they [other girls in class] sit away from me. I think, I think they don't like me because all the attention from TAs.

Some young people considered teaching assistants to hinder their learning in the classroom, as opposed to facilitating it. As Mike pointed out:

> I have a TA in class who writes it down [things from the board] but sometimes they don't write it down they just stop, I can't see the board and I expect the TAs to write it down but sometimes [they] just talk to my [peer] about football or something, so what I do is I get the book out and I put it in front of his face and like 'do it' because, you know, because it's, I'm not like telling them 'oh you have to do it' but it's their job isn't it.

Similar barriers were recognized by some educational professionals, who perceived them to be caused by disabling social structures rather than the individual's impairment. However, this attitude seemed to stem from personal experience or an interest in disability issues, rather than a whole school policy. For example, although four educational professionals were interviewed in one of the mainstream schools involved in the study, only one, a teacher who had a disabled wife, mentioned instances when support provision in the school was more of a hindrance than a help:

> Sam can't write his exam answers so he has a scribe in the exams. He did an exam in January and he had to explain a technical diagram to a scribe who is not business-trained. That was an absolute disaster. Sam got 7 out of 100 in the exam and it is not ability. It's the fact that he had to have a scribe. He said 'I knew the diagram and I got it in my head and I tried to describe to someone to draw a circle with lines coming out' but the scribe was not au fait with the situation. That was the real problem. He wants to go to [East Midlands] University. I'm going to write to them and say 'this exam result was because of the scribe'.

While the quality of support was not always suitable, the quantity of support was also perceived as a barrier to participation. Young people thought the amount of support they received over the years had been reduced, and was currently not enough for them to be fully involved in school life on a par with non-disabled peers:

I do have support and that, but now, more support goes to year 7 and I'm in year 10 so all the support is going to the year 7s and the year 8s … Would like a bit more but I'm leaving soon (Ikky, aged 15).

I don't get that much support as I did in year 7. (Tommo, aged 15)

A misuse of teaching assistants, cited by Ofsted (2004), is their role as replacement teachers for young disabled people. Young disabled people are often considered to be disruptive and difficult to educate (Barnes, Mercer and Shakespeare 2003) and thus are likely to be taught almost entirely by teaching assistants who are not fully qualified (Warnock 2005). For example, Jenny, a young person in a mainstream comprehensive, said: 'If I'm stuck [in class] I put my hand up and ask the TA.' This practice is supposed to take strain off teachers and enable them to work with non-disabled students so the school can meet national targets and normative comparisons. However, minimizing interaction between teachers and disabled students also goes against the government's drive to remove barriers to learning and increase teacher training in schools. Further, presenting young disabled people with sub-standard learning opportunities in school will cause subsequent inequalities in the adult labour market.

Friendships and Social Relationships

Friends were important to the young people, and they often identified them as their favourite thing about school. As mentioned above, for young people in special schools friends were considered one of the main reasons for their choice of post-school placement (to sixth form or college). This has also been noted by Cook, Swain and French (2001) and Vlachou (1997), who find that young people in special schools had strong social networks as well as a strong sense of belonging and inclusion.

Some of the young people in this study had experienced both types of schooling and they considered it easier to build friendships and social networks in special schools/colleges rather than mainstream schools. As Watson et al. (1999) suggest, special schools provide young disabled people with supportive environments, both physically and socially, in which they can explore and develop social relationships without the intervention of mainstream barriers. Roberts and Smith (1999) argue that structural and organizational arrangements in the school may prevent interactions between disabled and non-disabled peers. Further, they suggest that these barriers could increase the amount of effort required by non-disabled young people to interact with disabled peers and thus weaken their intentions to engage in such behaviour. This can be exemplified by Cathy's experiences of being in a Pupil Referral Unit (mentioned above) where she was separated from non-disabled peers. Hannah also experienced social isolation and several disabling barriers, at her mainstream school in Africa, which limited her opportunities to build friendships. When she moved to a special school in England at the age of 16, this changed:

> I did go to school for a while, but it, I had to be taken out, so I just lost touch with all my friends ... I was born out there [in Africa] so, and they didn't have the facilities that they've got here ... In this school I've finally got the chance to make friends and everything. I didn't have any friends when I lived in Africa.

Paul, who moved from mainstream secondary school to a special further education college, told a similar story: 'It's easier to make friends here [at special college] because people always come up and talk to you ... At my school [mainstream] it wasn't easy to make friends, I did have one friend but he left.'

Noalga moved from mainstream primary to special secondary school as a result of feeling excluded and not getting the support he required. He found the latter better in terms of building social relationships in and out of the classroom:

> We are all friends here, good friends [in special school], at my mainstream school I got picked on a lot because [they thought] I was funny looking ... I didn't have any friends there ... At my old [mainstream] school they [other kids] would not be my partner in sports lessons, they thought I can't do nothing and left me out.

A possible explanation for such interactions between disabled and non-disabled classmates is the lack of knowledge or skills concerning disability, rather than structural barriers. Roberts and Smith (1999) propose that providing non-disabled young people with more knowledge and practical skills about disability and impairment can influence their perceived control and their behavioural intentions. In other words, when non-disabled young people are equipped with relevant knowledge and skills about an issue unfamiliar to them, such as disability and impairment, they can feel more in control of their behaviour and choose more positive actions to interact with disabled peers.

Both Jane and Schumacher have been in special education from an early age although they had experienced mainstream school for a short period of time during their secondary education. They considered the supportive barrier-free environment of special education to be important for developing positive social relationships. The fact that every student at the specialist college had an impairment of some description meant that they were not worried about being singled out or being different, which they thought would be an issue in mainstream school:

> The one thing about special school is that we're all in the same boat and people don't look at you as if you've got four heads, I mean my brother's experienced bullying and all sorts because his sister [me] is different. (Schumacher, aged 20)

> I might have been the only one in a wheelchair you see and that wouldn't have been very, well it wouldn't have been very pleasant for me would it really? (Jane, aged 18)

However, although Jane was afraid of being seen as 'different' in a mainstream school, she also believed she had missed an opportunity to mix with non-disabled peers: 'I would have liked to have gone to one [mainstream school] in a way because I would be mixing with other people.'

This has been identified as a major problem of special schools which, due to being limited in number, require young disabled people to be transported out of their local community, away from non-disabled friends and family. Furthermore, young people miss out on participating in after-school activities with non-disabled children from their local area or from socializing with school friends at weekends and in the holidays (Shah, Travers and Arnold 2004a). The young people and teachers in special school confirmed this:

> We [school friends] do live quite far away from each other [so don't see each other outside school]. (Hannah, aged 18)

> I think it is just socially that they are affected in terms of them being taken away from the community. They build up social ties here but when they go home they can be more isolated because they haven't got those links in their local area, they haven't got friendships of a large peer group. They are fairly limited in the peer groups that they've got. So the social things that they do out of school are quite limited (Deputy Head and Careers Teacher, special school)

The young people based full-time at mainstream school reported how access limitations and attitudinal prejudice of mainstream school staff prevented them from building positive social relationships with non-disabled students and contributing to formal and informal learning:

> It's just hard at school 'cos they all [non-disabled pupils] go down the field and that's a bit stupid 'cos if they really want to see me and stuff they wouldn't go right down a grassy bank 'cos I'm not that stupid that I'd let my wheelchair go 'cos I'd tip down. (Sabrina, aged 14)

> I got into a comprehensive but it had a unit but I had to spend most of the time in and that was just like the special school ... I went to the occasional English, history, music, RE but it was occasional so by the time I went again I couldn't catch up because I had missed out on so much they didn't expect me to do the ordinary work. (Maggie, aged 19)

The young people's exclusion from school trips, due to lack of support or accessible transport, also limited their opportunities to develop social relationships with non-disabled peers. While some educationalists were aware of this problem, others were not. The following are different interpretations about this issue, presented from the viewpoints of a young disabled person and an educational professional from the same school. They illustrate the importance of consulting children and young people about issues concerning their lives, and not relying solely on adults' conceptions of childhood which, as concurred by Such, Walker and Walker (2005), are at best partial with limited connection to the views and experiences of children and young people:

> I haven't been allowed to go on some of the trips because they're not accessible to wheelchairs. (Sam, aged 17, mainstream school)

> Well they went to Germany but I generally didn't want to go, because it would have been hard and everything, I would have done but it was a bit hard so I didn't go. (Mike, aged 15)

> I'm not sure if any of our wheelchair users haven't been allowed to go on our trips. Since I've been here I think they've all gone on the trip but might not have accessed everything on the trip ...The Peak Surprise view in Derbyshire is the main one, it is just not wheelchair-accessible at all to get to the top to look at the peak. We have suggested to them to take a video camera (sixth formers go to lend a hand) and to film the views from the peak and to show it to those that are not able to go there. The bus companies we use should all be wheelchair-accessible. Sometimes if they've not been able to get on the bus we have had wheelchair users that have had to go with a teacher in the car – but they're not getting the atmosphere of being with all the friends on the bus. We've now got that list of bus companies and, touch wood, it will happen. (SENCO, mainstream school)

Such practices, created by non-disabled adults, to include young disabled people in schools could also serve to do the opposite in reality. According to young disabled people themselves, such practices not only prevent them from learning and making choices on a par with their non-disabled counterparts, but serve to create a divide between disabled and non-disabled peers by reinforcing the notion that disabled people are different, dependent, and in need of special resources and treatment: 'the bad thing is that I, I have to wait for people to open the door unless I try and do it myself, I can do a few doors myself but not all' (Sam, aged 17).

Vlachou (1997, 125) finds that young non-disabled people tend to view disabled peers as inferior, dependent and less competent. These perceptions are influenced by the special arrangements made for young disabled people in school: 'They've got special equipment and some special teachers that could help them to understand things and special computers so they know what they're doing.'

Given that the support and facilities available to accommodate diversity and maintain inclusivity in the classroom do not always do so, one can question the purpose of school policies and procedures implemented for young disabled people. While schools may strive to prepare young non-disabled people for successful economic adulthood (Cullingford 2002), it can be argued that this may not be the same for young disabled people who, as is evidenced above, can be excluded by the very policies intended to contribute to their inclusion.

Conclusion

Through the perspectives of young disabled people, this chapter has explored how the structures inherent in special and mainstream schools shape the choices young disabled people make for their subsequent future selves. It has considered the different ways in which mainstream and special education restrict and promote disabled young people's choices and opportunities to contribute to and participate in significant decisions that affect their life course. Presenting young disabled people as critical social actors, this chapter has identified issues that they think should be challenged within the education system so they have more opportunity to exercise their own choices and steer their own futures. The empirical data suggests that policies through which non-disabled adults aim to increase educational inclusion for young disabled people can also serve to disempower them by restricting their social and academic choices. Thus, such policies need to be redesigned after young disabled people themselves have been consulted.

Real inclusion should mean that there are genuine opportunities for all pupils to participate, to the best of their abilities, in all that school or college has to offer (Bishop 2001; Corbett 2001). However, the young disabled people identified several benefits and drawbacks of inclusion and segregated education, as it currently stands, and believed that no single type of placement could meet all the needs of all disabled students throughout their educational careers. Their experiences highlighted the issue of choice and how the limitations of both educational systems caused young disabled people to compromise their original aspirations. For instance, some young people identified the lack of academic orientation and limited curriculum of special schools as a problem in terms of restricting their learning opportunities and subsequent employment prospects. On the other hand they preferred the barrier-free environment of special schools, which promoted social acceptance, as opposed to the unsupportive environment of mainstream schools, even though they offered opportunities to follow individual aspirations. Other young people chose to put up with the physical and social barriers of mainstream education to ensure that they receive learning opportunities on a par with non-disabled peers. They saw special schools as reinforcing negative difference and isolating young people from the real world. This echoes work by BCODP and Barnes (1991) who argue that special education disables individuals from the realities of society. So in effect the future selves of young disabled people are not the result of their own decisions but the construction of disabling structures in education and society.

There is much support for advocates of inclusion, such as the Centre for Studies on Inclusive Education (CSIE), an independent centre working to promote inclusion and end segregation in the UK education system. CSIE argues that, as a fundamental issue of human rights, every child should have the right to attend a mainstream school in their local area. However, the reality is that a great deal of change is required within mainstream schools before disabled children will actually experience inclusion and be able to equally contribute and participate. It is suggested here, from the young people's experiences and views, that mainstream schools still have not embraced full inclusion and continue to disempower disabled students with exclusionary procedures and practices that could be intended to maximize their inclusion. These include the role of teaching assistants who have the potential to hinder as well as help. As Shaw (1998) argues, in order to get the right balance it is essential to involve young disabled people in negotiations and decision-making.

On a similar note, policies and legislation dictate disabled students' experience of work placements in terms of the extent to which these relate to the students' original choices. New legislation around child protection and safety has generated a risk-averse culture among employers, who are not obliged to accept disabled students for work experience as this is not covered by the Disability Discrimination Act in the same way as paid employment (Russell Commission 2005). Therefore students in special schools who have high-level support needs are either excluded from this learning opportunity or have to passively accept work placements that can guarantee support and access facilities. Where students have opportunities to do work experience in relation to career aspirations, this is not always successful due to limited access within mainstream educational or employment structures. So again, young disabled people are denied opportunities to fully participate in the development of their lives by disabling social structures and processes.

This chapter has presented different viewpoints from young disabled people who have real-life experiences of special and mainstream educational systems. Their accounts can be used to combat exclusionary practices and develop a new flexible system that offers the benefits of mainstream and special education, and facilitates young disabled people's self-determination in making choices about participating in and contributing to their independent futures.

Chapter 5

How Families Shape the Choices of Young Disabled People

The family plays a critical role in a child's development and choices made for adult life. It is one of the most influential social structures in society, moulding children and impressing them with certain expectations, values and beliefs that shape their aspirations and choices throughout the courses of their lives. This chapter explores the role of the family in shaping the career choices of young people. It reviews the literature that identifies which specific family characteristics influence the development of aspirations. It focuses particularly on how families encourage and discourage the pursuit of certain career routes, through the concepts of rules, beliefs, values, expectations, support and advice. Further it discusses the influence of parental occupation and thus, social class, on the generation of aspirations. Disabled children and young people may not be socialized in the same way as their non-disabled peers or siblings due to the influence of medical model thinking, which has left many families unsure of what to expect of disabled children, thus excluding them from many important patterns of socialization and social processes. This chapter presents empirical data from young disabled people, who tell stories of their relationships with parents and siblings, and how different family units shaped their aspirations and choices. This includes role modelling effects, parental expectations, family socio-economic background, parental occupations, and how strong identification with same-sex relatives influences the development of gender-typical aspirations. By listening to the views of young disabled people, families and government can learn how they can contribute to the full citizenship of young disabled people and their inclusion in mainstream society.

Introduction

The family is often considered to be the most influential agency in the socialization of the child. From a functionalist perspective, the family is a unit that performs certain specialized roles that contribute to society's basic needs and help to transmit information to children about the social and cultural order of the society in which they are born. Although family structures have evolved over time as a consequence of industrialization and changing society, Batcher (1982) argues that it is still a powerful emotional system that shapes and determines the individual's life course. While the impact of school, discussed in the previous chapter, does in fact influence young people's future selves, the family has been frequently described as more significant to the development of young people's aspirations and choices concerning educational and occupational trajectories (Cohen-Scali 2003; Roe 1956; Shah 2005a). Guichard (1993, 25) makes this clear:

> One insisted up to now on the place the school organization in the determination of intentions for future could hold. It is obvious that school is not the only institution which provides to the young adult frames enabling him to structure its professional intentions for the future. The family, the whole socially controlled experiences of the individual, play a role.

Families influence children's and young people's career-related interests in a number of ways. They are the first to communicate knowledge, representations and attitudes towards work and to shape children's preferences for certain careers. Dreams of parents and caregivers, whether successful or not, shape the career choices of their children (Jacobsen 2000). They provide valuable learning experiences, through acting as models, as well as by supporting or not supporting activities that assist young people in exploring a career choice of interest. Social learning theorists Bandura and Walters (1963), and Woelfel and Haller (1971) report that modelling is a powerful mode of social influence on career choices.

Further, it is within the family that young people master certain developmental skills considered essential to the construction of a professional identity (Cohen-Scali 2003). These include learning how to organize oneself, planning and accomplishing different projects and developing individual abilities. The abilities young people achieve, the choices they make and the type of projects they engage with are influenced by the context of whole family unit, including socio-economic status, the relationships between family members, parental expectations, family values and traditions. These issues can facilitate or restrict young people's horizons for action and pursuit of certain goals (Hodkinson, Sparkes and Hodkinson 1996).

Foskett and Hemsley-Brown (2001) contend that the choice process in middle-class families is predominantly concerned with guiding, shaping and ensuring choices are realistic in terms of being within individual's capabilities. Working-class families tend to delegate decision-making to children, especially if the decision is concerned with education, because parents perceive that their limited knowledge of the system would be a hindrance to children's progression (Reay and Ball 1998).

Social class also affects the types of jobs young people consider, influencing the choice of some careers and preventing the choice of others. Gottfredson (1981) argues that in most cases youngsters will take the group that they are a member of as their reference point when considering their occupational futures. So a working-class child is more likely to orient to typical working-class careers and adopt working-class standards for success. A middle-class child will orient to a middle-class career with its more demanding standards.

Research indicates pronounced differences between social class and ability level. Eysenck and Cookson (1970) reveal that high achieving children are encountered more frequently in more affluent families, where parents work in high-status occupations and the culture values hard work and encourages the achievement of high-flying goals. Shah (2005a) found social class background and parental occupation was also important to the career decisions and aspirations of disabled people. The work revealed that disabled people's aspirations are more a reflection of their socio-economic background than their disability status. This supports the argument that disabled people, like non-disabled people, are not a homogeneous group but have different social experiences, opportunities and relationships, that shape their choices and development.

As discussed in Chapter 4, disabling structures in society serve to limit the opportunities for disabled people to access opportunities in education and employment on a par with non-disabled peers. Together with the commonly held medical model view of disabled people being passive dependent recipients of charity unable to contribute to economic society, and the lack of positive disabled role models (Shah, Travers and Arnold 2004a), these societal structures have negative influences on parents' expectations of disabled children. The stories from a minority of young disabled people from this study reveal that negative expectations and lack of familial support sometimes have an adverse effect on their determination to pursue their aspiration.

Often, even where family members are unsure about what disabled children will be able to achieve, they do support them to meet their aspirations, acting as sources of information about educational and occupational opportunities (Shah 2005a). Nurturing children in a warm supportive environment and respecting them as valued individuals is important for the cultivation of individual potential. Hart (2008) contends that listening to what young people say and respecting their views has a positive impact on their sense of self.

The Influence of Families

As young people grow and develop, they are generally faced with the need to make important life choices, including decisions about their educational and occupational futures. As discussed in Chapter 3, choices and aspirations do not appear from nowhere: they are influenced by a variety of factors. Hargrove, Inman and Crane (2005) argue that young people's abilities to explore, consider and make career choices are significantly influenced by family boundaries, relationships and emotional interdependencies. According to Jacobsen (2000, 66), families provide offspring with: 'a vision of human life-what it means to be a good person: what constitutes success and failure, what our responsibilities are to ourselves and others'.

This is endorsed by Blair, Blair and Madamba (2003) who contend that, from an early age, children's choices, behaviour and actions will by affected by the familial context. Families provide children with a learning environment and direct and indirect knowledge, which they reflect on in future years. Families are often the source of initial career fantasies and career information, even when nuanced and subtle (Chope 2006). Vondracek, Lerner and Schulenberg (1986) have argued that learned roles and family expectations are likely powerful influences on vocational behaviour and this is supported by Michael Rutter (see Otto 2000, 111): 'Young people tend both to share their parents' values on the major issues of life and also turn to them for guidance on most major concerns' (1989).

A review of Latino-American literature by Whiston and Keller (2004) suggests that this varies according to race and class. Their analysis reveals that families had more of an effect on childhood career aspirations for some White ethnic groups than for others. Further, African-American and Latino college students were reported to consider parental support as valuable to their career development (Fisher and Griggs 1995; Fisher and Padmawidjaja 1999) but White ethnic students attributed less value to parental support (Dillard and Campbell 1981). This 'race' difference is rejected by Otto (2000) who finds that both young people from White and African-American ethnic backgrounds considered parents, especially mothers, to be positive resources in the process of their career development. In the current study with young disabled people, a comparison according to race could not be made due to the unrepresentative sample. Only two out of 33 young people identified themselves as being from non-White ethnic minority backgrounds, but they expressed similar experiences of growing up with a supportive extended family network, and within specific cultural values. Blair, Blair and Madamba (2003) argue that several elements of ethnic groups' specific values (for example, religion, language, family values) may affect children's aspirations in different ways, including the value they put on education, and the types of occupations they aspire towards. For instance, Asian culture values hard work and emphasizes the achievement of high standards in educational and occupational pursuits. Bignall and Butt (2000) find that young disabled people from ethnic minorities value education and see it as a stepping stone to a particular career. The young people from this study, Mike and Ikky, expressed a desire to get a good education to get the qualifications required to secure a good job:

> I've chosen French, IT, erm, English, science, maths, just the basic subjects because they're good for the career I want to do ... GCSEs next year ... then A Levels ... then University ... I need IT skills, communication skills because you have to interview people, um but qualifications, English is a big one, IT I need but I'm good at IT 'cos for typing it up and maybe maths to work out percentages and stuff. (Mike, aged 15)

I was gonna think of doing sport science and IT but then I wanted to keep IT from sports. I know it keeps you fit and that but IT is my main subject and I'm gonna get a job with IT ... I want to do IT and design software or like put programs on them, stuff like that ... to get a job that I'm wanting to get I'd need kind of a good qualification really 'cos if your looking for a good job you need a good qualification. (Ikky, aged 15)

Both young men were part of two-parent families and identified their family members, immediate and extended, as the most significant people in the construction and positive development of their future selves. As Brown (2004) has argued, the strong involvement of the extended family in directing children and adults has been viewed as reflecting the collectivistic cultures of Asian life. Hussain, Atkin and Ahmed (2002) point out, however, that young disabled people may not experience the same benefits from Asian family culture as their non-disabled contemporaries. Their work, with young disabled people from South Asian backgrounds, suggests that although parents want the best opportunities for their disabled children, the fact that they are too protective and have low expectations of what a disabled child can achieve hinders the young person's opportunities to achieve their goals. This is contrary to the current study, which finds that although a minority of young disabled people did mention opportunities being hindered by their parents' low expectations of them, these young people were from White ethnic families. The two young disabled people from Asian backgrounds considered their family to be significant to the development of their occupational preferences in a number of positive ways. Their narratives did not include anything about overprotective parenting or low expectations suppressing their development, but only of how their family supported and encouraged the young people's choices by transmitting relevant information about education and occupations, or by acting as role models.

Families as a Source of Support and Advice

In general, young disabled people in mainstream schools perceived their families as supportive of their aspirations, transmitting suitable information in relation to their educational and occupational choices. This supports the work of Pascall and Hendey (2004) who find that young disabled people identify their parents as key to their transition to adulthood. Wood (1973) asserts that where parents are warm, loving, respectful to their child as a valued individual, and able to enhance her/ his self-esteem, the child has the best opportunity to develop their personality to the full. Furthermore, the provision of such a nurturing environment permits the cultivation of individual potential. This parent-child relationship was evident in some of the young disabled people's narratives:

They were really like happy for me because I'm good at journalism I've done my magazine and they know that and I [always make them buy a copy] apart from that they're really like supportive ... they've always said it's up to you, um 'cos they know I'll pick a logical career anyway so they've always um known, they've always left it up to me like to make my own, like decision, but they always help, so if I said I want to be a journalist they'd help me like with telling me what qualifications you need and where I can get advice from, so they've never done it for me or like left me to do it all on my own. (Mike, aged 15)

My dad knows about it and my mum knows about it but, yeah they think it's for me ... they've said that whatever you're happy with, I'm happy with, so you can get on with what you want. (Ikky, aged 15)

Millie, who had aspirations to be a dancer, described her parents as supportive of her choices and said that it was her mother who sought and transmitted information about suitable dance training: 'They said I just should go along with what I want and my instincts and things like that ... hopefully I'm starting a drama school after school, my mum's still ringing up and get my place there but it's very booked up' (Millie, aged 13).

Similarly, Jenny, who loved performing arts at school and wanted to pursue a career in that area, perceived of her family as very encouraging of her ambition. They supported her by doing things like going to watch her perform in school shows and listening to her rehearse in her bedroom:

The dance shows are good, we do one or two a year. All my family came to see me ... They're always really supportive, sometimes when I'm in my room singing they've been listening at the door, I didn't know they were there. (Jenny, aged 14)

Sam was studying for his A Levels in preparation for going to university to pursue a degree connected with media and felt that his parents were supportive of whatever he chose to do. He felt his mother was particularly keen for him to go to university, as long as this was not too far from home: 'well my mum wants me to go to university and my dad doesn't mind what I do really he'll support [in whatever I do] and my mum wants me to go to X university because it's closer' (Sam, aged 17).

Similarly Steve's parents always supported his aim to do well at school and go to university. Both his parents worked in professional jobs and he was exposed to a culture of practices of hard work and doing well. There was an implicit expectation that Steve would also become qualified to work in his chosen profession. This supports work by Pascall and Hendey (2004), who find a connection between social class background and disabled people's levels of achievement. They suggest that parents who have inside knowledge have networks that can make great contributions to the achievements of their disabled children. Such is exemplified in this study. Steve's mother worked as a teaching assistant for disabled students in a mainstream school and thus had inside knowledge, resources and networks that may have helped to encourage and support his choices, as opposed to obstruct or change them in any way. As Priestley (1998) argues, disabled people socialized within middle-class socio-economic backgrounds have greater access to services and facilities than their working-class contemporaries. For instance, as Parish and Cloud (2006) suggest, children from professional two-parent families are more likely to receive care and attention from their own parents who are likely to have flexibility to arrange their work schedules to share childcare responsibilities. Further, as Shah (2005a) finds in a study of disabled high-flyers, although middle-class parents were aware of their child's impairment, they were unlikely to perceive it as a barrier to opportunity. This was evident in Steve's case. He believed his parents had confidence that he would not aspire to pursue goals beyond his means: 'it's always been a long-term aim to go [to university] ... I've always kind of concentrated on the things I know I can do, and erm, there won't be any problems with so...'

Several young people attending special schools also considered their parents to be supportive of educational and occupational aspirations. Fiona's family supported her decision to go to a specialist residential college, away from her home town, to pursue a course in photography: 'they're happy for me to go [to college] in a way. But, they'll miss us ... They've just encouraged me to do what I want.'

Similarly, Hannah, who wanted to be a photographer, initially received messages from her parents regarding what occupation they perceived as being most appropriate for her, but eventually they supported her own aspirations: '... I want to be a photographer and that's what I'm going to do. Now they've started supporting me a bit more.'

Bella had to reject her original goal of becoming a nurse as a consequence of disabling barriers, but felt her family were very supportive of her redirected goal to be a deaf youth worker:

> My family, my relatives I've told, and me grandma ... They thought it was very good that I was doing that, that I, um you know, wanted to work with them to help them [deaf people] ... my sister was very happy about me, but then when I told her I didn't want to do that [be a nurse] she wasn't disappointed, she just said do whatever you want, she's very pleased with me wanting to work with deaf people.

Although parents supported the young people's choices to do what they wanted to do and what made them happy, some thought their child's impairment would prevent them from being successful in their chosen career. Therefore they offered alternative occupations that they considered more suitable and congruent with their child's ability and impairment:

> I want to go to college to do either drama or media studies or computer studies ... I've talked to my parents. Personally they didn't think I could ... my dad wants me to work

with, umm, disabled people ... Like looking after them and stuff like ... But umm I want to do what I want to do, and I'll make sure I'll do it. (Nay, aged 14)

On a similar note, Hannah recalled how her dad tried to persuade her to work with computers as he perceived such a job would be easier for a wheelchair user than fashion photography: 'My dad seemed to think I should get a job with computers, but I didn't want it; I wasn't having it.'

Unsupportive Parents

However, other parents reinforced the stigmatizing cultural meaning attached to most impairments in mainstream society. They considered the young people's choices to be unrealistic, without offering any alternative. Tim, who had very limited movement in his legs, expressed a desire to be a coach driver. Although his father perceived this to be an unrealistic idea, Tim had not readily accepted this and believed there was a way he could achieve it:

> Me dad will say it's going to be a bit difficult so, um I've had a word with me dad actually about the coaching thing er, the only problem is the leg problem. And that is really a big problem but er I'm sure they will adapt. (Tim, aged 15)

Likewise Zoë, who lived in a single-parent family with an unemployed mother, had not been persuaded against following her aspiration to work with babies and children, despite her mother's lack of support:

> She [mum] always thinks I'm living in a dream world ... She says 'start living in the real world, don't live in a dream world', and I often think I'm not living in a dream world if I want to do it I can do it. Alright it might take me a bit longer to do it but I'm me own person, I'll do it. (Zoë, aged 17)

It can be argued that parents' attitudes towards their disabled children's occupational aspirations may have been influenced by the medical model perspective of disability, which attributes the problem and characterizes disabled children by narratives of dependence, vulnerability and exclusion (Priestley 1998). As the problem is perceived to be with the individual rather than with society, parents will tend to focus on how to fit their child into societal structures such as the labour market, as opposed to adapting structures to fit their child's choices. As Shah (2005a) argues, any preconceived expectations parents may have of their disabled children tend to be measured according to the child's level of impairment, and influenced by the implications of bringing up a disabled child in a predominately non-disabled world. This may be more prominent in single-parent or low-income families than middle-class families, as the former do not have the extra financial resources or time to invest in them. According to a review of research by the Joseph Rowntree

Foundation (Morris 1999), parents of disabled children face three times the costs of parents of non-disabled children. It finds that the average cost of bringing up a disabled child is £125,000 (£7,355 per year) in comparison with an average of £37,394 (£2,100 per year) for a non-disabled child. Further, according to an American study by Lee, Sills and Gi-Taik (2002), single mothers are more likely than two-parent families to have a disabled child. Sloper and Beresford (2006) suggest that many lone-parent families with disabled children live solely on state benefits because the childcare needs and lack of suitable alternative childcare affects parents' ability to work. However, despite the additional challenge of juggling employment with caring for a disabled child, Lee, Sills and Gi-Taik (2002) find that single mothers with a disabled child have a work participation rate which is only slightly lower than single mothers with non-disabled children. In the current welfare climate, many parents do not receive their full benefit entitlements, and even when they do they are not sufficient to meet the costs of bringing up a disabled child (Morris 1999), thus single mothers have little choice but to work to cover the costs. However, research has shown that this is detrimental to the well-being of the parent, the disabled child and the parent-child relationship (Lee, Sills and Gi-Taik 2002). Parents with disabled children suffer from higher levels of stress and lower levels of well-being than their counterparts with non-disabled children (Beresford and Sloper 2006). This could be caused by a number of factors including over-tiredness resulting from combining childcare with work, lack of resources to provide sufficiently for family needs and lack of support.

As Chope (2006) argues, families can restrict young people's career-related choices. One way they can do this is through their lack of or low expectations about what might happen in the future. Families with disabled children may develop low expectations of their child's future life based on subjective knowledge and communications with medical professionals who have knowledge of the child's medical condition (Russell 2003). These low expectations can affect a person's beliefs and how they behave during social interactions with others (Tajfel and Fraser 1978). For instance, in the current study, Zoë felt unsupported by her mother who seemed to have low expectations of her, reinforced by comments like 'start living in the real world'. However, Zoë was not discouraged by these comments. Rather, they made her stronger and more determined. Her mother's unemployment and present life situation had been significant to Zoë's choices and motivation in terms of teaching her what not to be like. Further the situation had possibly had a wounding effect on Zoë, but her self-belief, determination and the support of significant others may have helped her learn from the experience and become stronger instead of being dragged down by it (Shah, Arnold and Travers 2004b): 'I've said to her I'm not leading, I'm not leading the life you're leading, you're leading at the minute ... I always say I am going to do this; I am going to.'

Similarly, Nick had troubles with his family which were highly significant to his post-college choice of wanting to live independently, his primary aspiration at the time of interviewing:

> I'm trying to find some residence from here so I don't have to go back home, 'cos of technical, well, family difficulties, err, basically they didn't want me so I moved out ... Just want to get this housing bit sorted first 'cos it's a priority as it stands now.

Quentin, aged 15 and attending special school, lived with his mother and younger brother. He did not express any particular aspiration for his subsequent future, or did not mention his family in relation to shaping his choices. When prompted to talk about his family, Quentin commented on how his family are often not at home when he finishes school, thus engendering feelings of neglect and isolation. He confessed that this was the thing he hated: 'I most hate going, when the house is empty, I hate going home to an empty house so.'

This suggests that there is a relationship between low socio-economic status, detached parenting styles and young people's lack of aspirations. McLoyd (1990) argues that low socio-economic status often engenders economic stress, in turn leading to unsupportive and hostile parenting practices which have been found to be negatively related to career aspirations (McDonald and Jessell 1992; McWhirter, Hackett and Bandalos 1998). However, it can be argued, as mentioned before, that some lone mothers with disabled children have no choice, due to unmet service needs, but to go to work to meet the cost of bringing up disabled and non-disabled children. Further, leaving children to supervise themselves may be the only option for some parents, given the obstacles associated with securing childcare provision for young disabled people. For example, few nurseries or child-minders are based in physically accessible buildings and many are unlikely to be managed by staff with appropriate training and expertise (Kagan, Lewis and Heaton 1998).

Lower socio-economic levels may limit the type of information available to youths about career options, affect the quality of educational opportunities and the availability of role models (Conger et al. 1993; Schulenberg, Vondracek and Crouter 1984). This is especially the case for young disabled people, who may often be excluded from mainstream childcare, play and leisure services (Azaad 1994) due to buildings or transport being unaffordable or physically inaccessible. Excluding disabled children and young people from mainstream play and leisure environments limits their opportunities to interact with non-disabled peers and obtain information and experiences to shape career aspirations and other life choices. It also puts pressure on single parents, presenting them with the dilemma of being full-time unemployed carers on welfare benefits that do not compensate for the cost of disability and loss of earnings, or being involved in paid work and in danger of appearing unsupportive and neglectful of their disabled child. Although there is no explicit data in this study to support this, it is possible that Quentin's 'latch-key kid' experience could have been influenced by the aforementioned dilemmas, which in turn had a blurred effect on his prospective choices. As Parish and Cloud (2006) contend, lack of parental care has some negative effects on the child's development in terms of generating adverse developmental outcomes, and the potential for suffering emotional harm.

Alternative Supports

Although Quentin did not mention his family in relation to shaping his life course in a positive way, his narrative suggests that he had alternative agents of social influence, namely his link worker who provided him with the support and role modelling effects other young people received from their families: 'I like going out with my link worker ... he takes me out every other weekend ... To town, the library or bowling ... does reading with me and that ...I'm a James Bond fan and so is he.'

This was similar for Zoë and Tyson who both lived in single-parent families with unemployed mothers who, they perceived, were unsupportive of their aspirations. Like Quentin, the young women both identified alternative support networks and significant others who influenced the development and pursuit of their individual choices. Tyson was restricted by the fact that she could no longer rely on her mother to provide her with the practical support she required to become involved in a Saturday drama group to get the experience of leading drama workshops:

> I used to lead them; due to my family changes I got taken out ... I left due to mum's health, that's what I left for ... it was too much commitment on a Saturday morning ... mum is basically getting old. Right with her having cancer at a very like difficult point in my life.

However, this unfortunate life event did not discourage her aspiration because she got support and encouragement from other sources. For example, she identified two teachers who she felt supported her choices and understood her situation:

> One of the teachers who's left now, he got connections that's how I got to know about it [the Saturday drama group].

> Mrs T [drama teacher] says you have not got a label; just because you're in wheelchair you are not labelled.

Zoë, whose mother told her to 'stop living in a dream world', mentioned teachers and peers as significant to her choices, in terms of supporting her and encouraging her to pursue them: 'Friends, 'cos they've then seen me with children they often, they often say to me do you want to get a job here?'

Family as Models

Another way in which families influence aspirations is by example. Role models are important in shaping young people's future expectations about their occupational choices. According to Kidd (1984) role models influence by direct communication and interaction, informing the young person about the occupational role in terms of what is involved and the extent to which their person specifications will match the requirements of the occupational role. Jans (2003) suggests that it is through role modelling effects that young people develop a sense of their own potential, self-esteem, awareness of a variety of careers and realistic expectations about possible challenges. However, Jans also argues that young disabled people may lack frequent exposure to disabled people in work and careers. Although they can be greatly inspired by non-disabled parents or siblings, non-disabled people will not be able to impart information about what it will be like to grow up as a disabled adult (Shah, 2005a). In the current study, Zoë, who could not identify with her mother and her low expectations, thought it was very important for young people like herself to see disabled adults in top jobs:

> I always say I am going to do this [work with children] ... I can do it 'cos one of my friends has got a disabled sister-in-law. She's a lot worse off than me. I've never met her but I can picture her. And she's working for a very rich company apparently ... every year there's disabled person working in the outreach office.

Other young people in the study, especially girls, were interested in the disabled researcher's biography in terms of how she had achieved her goals and overcome disabling barriers set to hinder her trajectories. For these young disabled people the researcher was a model who could share insightful experience about how to achieve personal and professional choices in a disabling world. This thirst for learning about the disabled researcher's life course could possibly be triggered by the lack of positive disabled role models available to young disabled people. Further, it is possible that the only information they may receive about growing up with an impairment is based on medical model stereotypes of disabled people being passive, dependent and different, and not on the actual positive real lives of disabled people. This lack of positive disabled role models may be a barrier to young disabled people having high expectations for themselves and developing a positive self-concept (Jans 2003).

Noalga was the only young person in this study who had a disabled family member. His older brother had the same impairment as he did and had attended the same special school two years earlier. At the time of interview he was studying multimedia at a local further education college. Noalga considered his brother as a role model, and was going to follow his example: 'my brother came here [school] before me. Now he is doing multimedia at college. He has inspired me to do that too after X school.'

In this case there were also same-sex role modelling effects in operation. This supports White, Cox and Cooper's (1992) theory that, in many cases, the older sibling is viewed by the younger as stronger, more competent and capable of executing relevant behaviour to meet his aspired goals. They suggest that the younger sibling is likely to adopt similar behaviour to the older sibling in order to achieve similar goals.

Other young disabled people's narratives also suggested effects of same-sex role models and significant sibling relationships. However, this was with non-disabled members of their family who were considered to play an important role in the development of the young people's subsequent occupational preferences. For instance, Ikky was inspired by same-sex relatives, particularly his cousin and uncle who both work in the field of IT and his older brother who studies IT. These relatives influenced Ikky's choices by their example:

> I heard from my cousin from London, he's like, he's an IT expert, I think he's like one expert [on a team] ... he says the money is good, he can fix computers, any problem they've got with computers.

> My uncle [gave me the idea of becoming an IT expert] ... he is ... he did get a good qualification.

> I've got one older brother ... he goes to college, does IT the same.

The young disabled people talked about a number of different ways siblings influenced their career aspirations, including being a role model, or supporting their choices by assisting with/participating in certain activities with them. For instance, Xavier, who was a big fan of computer games, mentioned his aspiration to his younger brother: 'my brother knows that I like doing games and stuff like that 'cos he's a fan of games as well ... we play two player games all the time. Except he always beats me.'

Similarly Jenny, who wanted to pursue a career in performing arts, said 'I do drama and a bit of singing with my sister.' Mike, who wanted to be a journalist, ran the school magazine with his younger brother: 'Um, well it's me and my brother run it [school magazine], well he just says he runs it but I run it properly and he's trying to sack me at the moment.'

This is consistent with Small and McClean's (2002) research: they report a marked gender effect with same-sex relatives having a greater influence on young people's life courses. Further work by Ouchman (1996) and Trankina (1992) suggests that same-sex role models have a more positive impact on self-esteem than other-sex role models. Bochner (1994) reports that same-sex models are particularly influential to adolescents' choices in later life despite their significant attraction to the opposite sex. However, as Wohlford, Lochman and Barry (2004) argue, males are more likely to choose same-sex role models than females because there are fewer available same-sex role models, particularly in high-status occupations, for women than for men.

This research shows that several of the young disabled people identified with same-sex relatives, including parents, siblings and extended family from varied ethnic backgrounds. Sabrina and Bella, both from a White ethnic background, were inspired by female members of their extended family. Sabrina's aspiration to be a language interpreter in French and Spanish stemmed from her close relationship with her aunt who went to university in France and speaks French:

> Why do I want to do it? ... I find the French language very good um very interesting, better then the English language ... my aunty is very very good in French she went to university in France so, she's good she's very good ... I would like to go to university in France ... my uncle passed away but my aunty still lives nearby, I see her quite a lot.

However, Sabrina also spoke about being inspired by her uncle who was Spanish. Bella's childhood dream to become a nurse was inspired by her sister-in-law who worked in the profession: 'when I was little I wanted to do nursing ... my sister-in-law is a nurse, so that's why I wanted to do, follow in the family [role] ...'

However, apart from Sabrina and Bella, no other females in this study considered female family members as role models. There was more direct linkage between fathers' occupations and boys' aspirations. A number of the males in the sample perceived their fathers as role models and had career aspirations that were significantly associated with their father's professional job status. A large body of literature suggests that children aspire to the careers of their parents at rates significantly above chance (Holland 1962; Werts and Watley 1972). Trice et al.'s (1995) work explains this as an effect of children being concurrently exposed to situations and talk related to parental work. Experiences such as helping parents with work-related problems and having personal involvement in their occupations are considered to have a crucial influence on young people's career aspirations (Chope 2006). The influence of a father's occupational status over their son's subsequent choice is not recent. As Blau and Duncan (1967) contend, a father's occupational status not only influences his son's career achievements by affecting his education and first job, but it also has a delayed effect on achievements that persist over the life course. A number of young males in this study were greatly influenced by their father's professional status and strived to do something similar. For example, Joe had an aspiration to fix heaters like his father: 'I want to work with my dad, fixing people's heaters ... I want to work in dad's store, when he wants me he presses 24 and I pick up the phone and say "hello P stores" and I write things down.'

Similarly Harry, who had redirected his goal from building computers to designing websites, developed an initial interest in computers as a consequence of his father's profession: 'I live with my dad, he's good with computers ... My dad's a computer analyst and puts all the err, programs on a computer.' Allan's father was also a computer analyst 'for the X bank'. Although not explicit, Allan's narrative suggested that his father's occupation may have had some influence on his aspiration to work in 'something to do with computer games'.

Mothers were perceived as having more of a supporting and caring role. This echoes Blair, Blair and Madamba's (2003) work which found that, among Asian and White families with non-disabled children, fathers were likely to influence their children's aspirations more substantially than mothers. It is possible that the girls in this study did not identify mothers as directly influential to their aspirations (as role models) because many were housewives and not employed. However, as mentioned previously, mothers of disabled children are often deterred from seeking employment due to the lack of sufficiently flexible work which would allow them to respond to family needs. Further young disabled people are likely to encounter more barriers and inequalities than their non-disabled peers, in their transition to adulthood, and thus there is a tendency for them to remain with their family for longer (Hendey 1999). Despite New Labour's policies to increase child benefits which can be used to buy childcare for non-disabled children, mothers of disabled children still face obstacles to taking employment because of the lack of support for young disabled people beyond school. As one parent put it:

> I think he's going to need that kind of help for longer ... for later than most children do, and I don't know how that will go, because now he's nearly 12, he's started secondary school. In another sort of year or so you'd expect that most kids would just come home with a key for the two or three days and that it would be reasonably safe, but we're not sure how that will go yet. (Kagan, Lewis and Heaton 1998, 3)

This problem has been recognized by the National Service Framework, a strategy which supports the Every Child Matters (DfES 2003) programme. The Framework recommends that disabled children and young people receive appropriate services that meet their needs and enable their families to live 'normal' lives.

Conclusion

This chapter has explored, through the lens of teenagers with physical impairments, how family structures have influenced their aspirations and choices for their future selves. Analysis has revealed that family history, socio-economic and cultural background and relationships with individual family members have a significant impact on the development of the young disabled people's education and career-related aspirations.

The work above suggests that, as for non-disabled people, the culture and socio-economic status of the family has a marked effect on progression and trajectories of young disabled people. Although Hussain, Atkin and Ahmed (2002) found Asian families with disabled children practiced over-protective parenting that became oppressive and obstructing, this study presents evidence to suggest that the support and involvement of extended family, in a culture which prizes hard work and high-status achievement, can have significant positive effects on the future vision of young disabled people. Families were perceived as providing necessary support and advice in relation to education and career goals.

Furthermore, families provided powerful role modelling effects. Several young people identified with same-sex family members in particular educational and occupational environments. However, most of the role models were not disabled and therefore did not have the insight and understanding about how to achieve professional and personal goals while growing up in a disabling society. The lack of positive disabled role models poses a problem for young disabled people aspiring to meet their goals while maintaining a positive disability identity (Jans 2003). Without the right information and guidance about how to negotiate barriers to achieve successful adulthoods, young disabled people may be in danger of conforming to the passive dependent image of a disabled person traditionally conveyed by medical model interpretations of disability.

Class appeared to have a significant effect on parents' perceptions of what their child could or could not achieve. The young people's narratives suggested single-parent low-income families were unsupportive of their aspirations, and indeed sometimes this was perceived as a potential barrier to progression. However, these perceived unsupportive parenting styles could be attributed to the barriers encountered by single parents with disabled children who have diminished earning power due to truncated or delayed benefit entitlements, and having to combine caring for their disabled child with working to cover the high cost of living with impairment and disability. This pressured situation inevitably results in a poor quality of life for low-income families (parents and disabled children alike) and thus a negative perception of disability. This research has identified the importance of families in the development of young disabled people's career aspirations. However, sometimes families themselves require support from professionals, be it emotional, physical or financial, before they can support their disabled child. Although some efforts are being made, under the Common Assessment Framework for Children and Young People, to provide professional input to families with disabled children, there is a call for more multi-agency working to ensure families' needs regarding housing and health are assessed.

own identities within the school context. These are not the passive, vulnerable children of the Dickensian novel or the socio-medical research literature.'

Therefore a strategy for change might be to encourage disabled people into high-status professions and avoid looking at impairment as a negative factor. This book is written from a social model perspective, as it identifies the social, environmental and attitudinal structures within young disabled people's education and family, which facilitate or prevent their imagined occupational futures becoming real futures.

Education and Employment

Young disabled people make it clear when talking about their education and career-related choices that they have similar aspirations to non-disabled young people. They do not expect to be dependent citizens in their adulthood, as popular rhetoric suggests. Their stories do emphasize the impact social structures have on the extent to which their aspirations are facilitated or constrained over time. For example, current educational opportunities for young disabled people are fraught with barriers that cause young disabled people to compromise their aspirations. Educational policies for disabled children are driven by non-disabled professionals who make important decisions about the education of disabled children without consulting them. This book has shown, through the insider voices of the young disabled people, that educational systems as they currently stand are not suited to the needs of all young disabled people throughout their educational careers. Young people's experiences in mainstream and special schools highlight structures that constrain their horizons for action, thus impeding their opportunities to actively contribute to and participate in choices and trajectories that allow them to live their future lives as equals to their non-disabled colleagues.

Disabled students were well aware of the drive towards educational inclusion as an alternative to special education. While they recognized that special education denies young disabled people opportunities to follow normal transitions and restricts their career choices due to a truncated curriculum and limited academic expertise of teachers, some young disabled people considered the supportive barrier-free environment of special education to be a preferable option to mainstream education. These young disabled people had negative experiences of mainstream education that inevitably shaped their views and attitudes towards it, causing them to retreat to special school where, in the short term, structures seemed less oppressive. So, despite the government's drive towards educational inclusion for all students and the practices employed by non-disabled professionals to increase the participation of disabled students in mainstream schools' life, this book presents young disabled people's voices of experience that tell stories of the extent to which these practices work in reality. The young people highlight drawbacks with recent practices, such as the use of teaching assistants, Pupil Referral Units and the physical infrastructure of mainstream schools that excluded, rather than facilitated, them from engaging in the social and academic opportunities on a par with their non-disabled peers. Such practices served to reinforce the disabled/non-disabled divide. So the material presented in this book demonstrates the impact that failing to involve young disabled people in changes and developments that affect their lives has on their future success as equal citizens and in society as a whole. It evidences the importance of getting young people's feedback about education and schooling to assess the 'success' of different programmes and policies. Without documentation of young people's experiences of education and schooling, policies might be misleading. As Philpott and Sait (2001, 13) point out, 'admittance without acceptance is not inclusion'.

Involving children in decision-making also has a positive impact on self-esteem and confidence. As Hart (2008) argues, if children/young people feel they are being listened to and their opinion is valued, they are more likely to develop a positive sense of self and feel encouraged to engage in social, academic and economic activities, thus integrating themselves as equal citizens within the mainstream community. Furthermore, this integration facilitates the growth of awareness and acceptance of disability among others. According to Sutherland (1981), acceptance becomes easier the more one conforms to the norm of the societal majority. This is supported by Reiser (1995) who argues that integration can benefit all young people and encourage them to develop into adults who accept and value diversity. Similarly Taylor and Palfreman-Kay (2000) contend that integration encourages the formation of social relationships between disabled and non-disabled children, closing the divide between them and dispelling any myths or fears of disabled children being different.

Chapter 4 of this text has highlighted the contrasting perspectives of non-disabled professionals and young disabled people on issues concerning the education of disabled people. According to young disabled people, the very structures created to empower them to participate in mainstream schooling are disabling and disempowering, restricting their freedom to explore and develop choices and relationships. Furthermore, support in mainstream education is haphazard and largely depends on local education authorities funding remits rather than disabled students' needs. Moreover, the cost of inclusion is causing the government to question what is financially less draining: sending disabled children away to special school or buying in resources to fit the mainstream school around the needs of the child. Although some young people expressed a preference for special education in terms of the support they received and the social relationships they could develop, they were still limited by the structures of the system which encouraged them to compromise their choices, which could delay their life course and emphasize their differences to non-disabled peers.

Segregating disabled and non-disabled children in their early years will lead to the latter developing into adult employers unable to value disability or difference in their workforce, thus perpetuating the same segregation and truncated opportunities over the life course.

Young disabled people are interested in working in a very wide range of occupations. They criticize lack of academic opportunities, including work experience, which constrain their opportunities to compete on a par with non-disabled colleagues in the global labour market. It is not only necessary to change education for young disabled people, but also the partnerships between education and employment institutions, so young people have more opportunities to test out their career aspirations through relevant work experience placements.

Currently the Disability Discrimination Act (2005) does not cover work experience so employers are likely to avoid taking a disabled student on a work placement. Young people requiring adaptations to, or support in, the workplace, while on their placement, are also not entitled to Access to Work as are full-time paid employees. Changing this policy would not only benefit young disabled people, by providing them with a forum to test out their aspirations and abilities, but also reduce the disabled/non-disabled divide by including all young people in learning activities, not just a minority. Further it would help to increase employers' awareness of disability issues, bridging the gap between societal stereotypes of disability and the reality, smoothing the transition of young disabled people into employment.

Taking the perspectives of the young disabled people involved in the production of this book, it is evident that they are not a homogenous group. They have different wants, needs and voices. Their rich accounts and individual experiences of disabling barriers and enabling structures in special and mainstream educational systems can be used to inform the development of a new flexible education system that would enhance the learning resources available to young disabled people, thus widening their horizons for action and opportunities to undergo life course transitions at the same rate as their non-disabled peers. This should, in turn, contribute to the reduction of significant inequalities which cause disabled people to live marginalized adulthoods.

Gender and Identity

In this study it became evident that the young disabled people felt gender had a substantial influence on their aspirations, more than disability status. Just under two-thirds of young people aspired to gender-typical careers. This is important to note given that disabled children's identities are often conceived of as one-dimensional: as a disabled person with no gender, sexuality, ethnicity or class. Many of the young disabled people identified same-sex role models who inspired their career-related decisions and supported their development. Therefore it is clearly evident that these young people have a positive gender identity themselves. However, it is up to society to ensure this is not lost by disabling barriers which cause disabled people to be perceived as genderless. As Priestley (2003) points out, disabled children and young people are often grouped into categories according to impairment definitions or labels for the convenience of service providers. This ascribed status identifies the child/young person according to their impairment above other attributes of their self-concept, such as gender, ethnicity and social class. One way to promote the gender and sexuality of disabled people could be via the media, by including disabled males and females into mainstream storylines, having social and sexual relationships typical of their gender. This may offer greater opportunities for disabled people to be viewed in terms of their multiple identities rather than just their impairment. Another method would be to show positive representations of disabled fashion models in magazines, in shops and on television. Ensuring physical access into shops and public transport would encourage young disabled people to choose their own clothes and go shopping with friends instead of relying on adults to make their choices for them and risking having their gender identity diluted by neutral sensible outfits chosen for them.

Family Relationships

Family structures have been evidenced as having a crucial impact on the life choices and chances of the younger generation: disabled and non-disabled. In this and other work, nationally and internationally (for example, Pascall and Hendey 2004; Philpott and Sait 2001; Shah 2005a), the role of parents is critical in determining whether a disabled child has hope, expectations and aspirations, and the resilience to overcome barriers they may encounter over their life course. In this book, the young disabled people identified their families as significant to the cultivation of their educational and career-related aspirations, in terms of providing sound support and advice, and powerful role modelling effects. However, it was clear from the young people's narratives that their non-disabled families did not expect them to grow up like them. Parents could not offer insightful advice about how to achieve professional and personal goals while growing up in a disabling society. The only advice parents tend to get about disabled children is based on medical model interpretations of disability that portray disabled people as passive and dependent non-contributing citizens. This suggests a fundamental need for positive disabled role models, not only for young disabled people but also so that non-disabled families can understand what the issues are for a child growing up to be a disabled adult, and how to negotiate barriers and oppression. Further, parents of disabled children need support not only to be able to perform their parental role effectively, that is to nurture and encourage the well-being of their disabled child, but also to maintain good health and relationships with other family members. The problems facing families of disabled children have been recognized in government reports including the major green paper *Every Child Matters: Change for Children* (DfES 2003) and the Cabinet Office report *Improving the Life Chances of Disabled People*, which aim to bring together a number of strategies and policies to improve outcomes for disabled children, young people and their families. These include the provision of the Disabled Facilities Grant, a non-means tested grant that assists with the costs of living with, and bringing up, a disabled child; and the Individual Budgets programme that builds on successful aspects of the Direct Payment Scheme with a view to providing disabled people with greater choice and control over their receipt of public services in terms of what they receive and when and how it is provided. Annual increases in the Carer's Grant also demonstrate the government's commitment to supporting families with disabled children, especially low-income lone-parent families who face increasing dilemmas between caring for their disabled child and avoiding living in poverty. Furthermore it should ensure that disabled children receive suitable skilled childcare, thus reducing the need for them to look after themselves, which is likely to pose great risks to their well-being, as was discussed in Chapter 5.

In the research discussed in the preceding chapters, social class differences reflected varieties in lifestyles including access to support and services, educational and social histories, and the expectations parents had of their disabled children. Social class also influenced the extent to which families constrained or encouraged the young people's choices and development. Young disabled people from two-parent families identified their families as their primary support network. However, a minority of young people in single-parent low-income families suggested that their family structures presented barriers to their development and were unsupportive of their choices. These perceived unsupportive parenting styles could be attributed to the barriers encountered by single parents with disabled children. Such barriers include diminished earning power caused by truncated or delayed benefit entitlements, and the need to combine caring for their disabled child with working to cover the high cost of disability due to limited support from relations. Additionally some parents need to work for their own mental well-being as well as out of financial necessity.

There is a danger that disabled children and their families will be caught in a perpetual poverty trap. When disabled children grow into disabled adults they are still faced with a wide range of additional living costs that include housing adaptations, transport and personal assistants: disabled people encounter significant barriers that limit their opportunities to achieve the same economic prospects as their non-disabled peers. According to the report *Monitoring Poverty and Social Exclusion*, by Palmer, McInnes and Kenway (2006), disabled people who rely solely on benefits experience a shortfall of £200 a week in the figure required to ensure a minimum standard of living. In both full-time and part-time employment, employees with a work-limiting disability are paid approximately 10 per cent less than employees without a work-limiting disability (Palmer, Carr and Kenway 2005). Disabled people are also less likely than their non-disabled colleagues to receive training or promotion opportunities. Therefore it is necessary to recognize and address issues that trap disabled people in poverty from the cradle to the grave.

As mentioned in Chapter 5, new initiatives are being introduced to meet the needs of families of disabled children. Organizations such as Contact A Family, founded in 1979, have been established to provide families of disabled children with information about where to get support and advice. However, recent evidence (see Sloper and Beresford 2006) shows that the profile of disabled children in the United Kingdom is changing and the needs of families with a disabled child are often unmet by existing child policies and health service practices. This calls for a greater understanding of the support required for young disabled people and their families to meet economic, educational and social aspirations and not be held back by disabling barriers. For such an understanding to be attained, disabled children and disabled adults need to be involved in the monitoring and evaluation of services. By listening to young disabled people, we learn what they want, need, enjoy and fear. Therefore this book could be a valuable resource for policy-makers, practitioners and parents who can hopefully be inspired by the young disabled people's stories and take account of what they are saying when developing policy and processes in their names.

The Last Word

The final question in the interviews with the young people was 'If you were given the power to change anything in the world, what would it be?' Their responses can be divided into two categories: societal and individual.

A few of the young people were keen to change things at an individual level, in relation to their impairment, thus adopting a medical model perspective. For instance, Allan who was 13 years old and attending a mainstream school, had gradually become a full-time wheelchair user as a consequence of a deteriorating muscle wasting condition that caused his legs to slowly weaken and eventually stop functioning. When asked what he would change, he said it would be his '...

ability to walk again, that'd be so good. I walked until year 2 then stopped, as it wasn't convenient.'

Similarly Harry, also a wheelchair user, recalls how he was ambulant before a hip dislocation:

> I used to be able to walk … got CP, I used to go to the school that would exercise my muscles and stuff … I used to be able to walk through parallel bars … but because my hip's gone, … I'd like to change it back into being able to walk.

Jenny, like Allan and Harry, had lost her ability to walk although still had a positive recollection of these times. If she could turn back the clock she would have liked to 'not to be in a wheelchair; I used to in my old school walk around on crutches but I had a hip operation and it went wrong so now I'm always in a wheelchair.' However, unlike Allan and Harry, Jenny's quote suggests that there is a need to change healthcare services and treatment, rather than herself, to achieve her goal.

Changing society to reduce inequalities and disabling barriers was reflected in many of the young disabled people's 'ideas for change'. Their last words referred to how they would like things to change at a societal level which could make an informed contribution to the development of policy for all young disabled people, not just themselves.

Sabrina, aged 14, had been a victim of disability-related prejudice and discrimination from young people and adults within and outside the school environment. She adopted a social model perspective in that she strongly believed that members of society should function together to succeed, as opposed to segregate people into minority groups: 'I would join up White and Asian people together as a unit.' Further, she perceived discrimination such as disablism to be a problem of societal attitudes rather than individual attributes and thus would have liked a society where:

> … people do not look down on people with disability … 'cos I don't think I could change my disability … The attitude towards disabled people isn't that great at the moment … like, those people, as you walk by, go 'ah bless her' and that really gets on my nerves 'cos they think you're like paralysed but we're not, we're gonna fight back.

Hannah, aged 18, and Schumacher, aged 20, also felt that there was an urgent need to change public attitudes to disability and impairment to enable young disabled people to achieve full citizenship on a par with their non-disabled peers in mainstream society:

> [I would] change people's attitudes probably … if I went shopping people would talk to the person that I was with and ignore me, they'd say like 'how old is she?' and I'd feel like saying 'I can talk you know'. (Hannah)

> It would be the way me and my friends are all looked at … For example, in my town at home I've had lots of people come up, just stand and look at me, and I'm like 'do you have a question for me?' and they're like 'no'. (Schumacher)

Several of the young people had insider perspectives on special and mainstream education, which they explored in presenting ideas about how to move to a more physically, socially and educationally inclusive system for themselves and other disabled students:

> I would change mainstream schools to make it better for other kids by having more staff, more helpers who know about disability, they could go on lifting and handling courses. Also there should be more accessible toilets. (Cathy, aged 14)

> I suppose that I would make sure that sort of disabled people get um an absolute equal chance to able-bodied people um that young people get educated about disabilities better in school. (Sam, aged 17)

> I know this sounds a bit weird but instead of lifts in this school, I think they should have ramps … because like lifts go two miles an hour as it is and you get, get to your lesson really, really late. (Nay, aged 14)

Finally, Mike closes this book with the following message:

> I'd make it easier for any disabled person not to feel as left out and excluded, because we're not freaks or anything, we're just the same [as non-disabled people] except they haven't got as much um, you know, they haven't got as much limitations.

Bibliography

Abberley, P. (1999), *The Significance of Work for the Citizenship of Disabled People* (Dublin: University College).

Abrams, F. (2004), *Inclusion is Just an Illusion* (London: TES) <http://www.tes.co.uk/search/story/?story_id=2047918>

Adams, M. and Brown, S. (eds) (2006), *Towards Inclusive Learning in Higher Education: Developing Curricula for Disabled Students* (London: Routledge).

Adams, M. and Holland, S. (2006), 'Improving Access to Higher Education', in M. Adams and S. Brown (eds). *Towards Inclusive Learning in Higher Education: Developing Curricula for Disabled Students* (London: Routledge).

Aiken, M., Ferman, L. and Sheppard, H. (1968), *Economic Failure, Alienation and Extremism* (Ann Arbor, MI: University of Michigan Press).

Alderson, P. and Goodey, C. (1998), *Enabling Education: Experiences in Special and Ordinary Schools* (London: The Tuffnell Press).

Allan, J. (1996), 'Foucault and Special Educational Needs: A "Box of Tools" for Analysing Children's Experiences of Mainstreaming', *Disability and Society* 11:2, 219–33.

Arbona, C. (1989), 'Hispanic Employment and the Holland Typology of Work'. *Career Development Quarterly* 37, 257–68.

Astin, H.S. (1984), 'The Meaning of Work in Women's Lives: A Sociopsychological Model of Career Choice and Work Behaviour', *Counselling Psychologist* 12, 117–26.

Aston, J., Willison, R., Davis, S. and Barkworth, R. (2005), *Employers and the New Deal for Disabled People: Qualitative Research, Wave 2; Research Report 231 – Department of Work and Pensions* (Leeds: Corporate Document Services).

Audit Commission (2002), *Special Needs: A Mainstream Issue* (London: Audit Commission).

Azaad, J.A. (1994), *The Road to Freedom* (York: Race Equality Unit).

Baldock, J., Manning, N. and Vickerstaff, S. (eds) (2003), *Social Policy* (Oxford: Oxford University Press).

Ball, S.J., Bowe, R. and Gerwitz, S. (1994), 'Market Forces and Parental Choice', in S. Tomlinson (ed.), *Educational Reform and its Consequences* (London: Institute for Public Policy Research and Rivers Oram Press).

Ball, S.J., Maguire, M. and Macrae, S. (2000), *Choice, Pathways and Transitions Post-16. New Youth, New Economies in the Global City* (London: Routledge Falmer).

Bambra, C., Whitehead, M. and Hamilton, V. (2005), 'Does Welfare-to-Work" Work? A Systematic Review of the Effectiveness of the UK's Welfare-to-Work Programmes for People with a Disability or Chronic Illness', *Social Science and Medicine* 60:9, 1905–18.

Bandura, A. (1977), *Social Learning Theory* (Englewood Cliffs, New Jersey: Prentice Hall).

Bandura, A., Barbaranelli, C., Caprara, G.V. and Pastorelli, C. (2001), 'Self-Efficacy Beliefs as Shapers of Children's Aspirations and Career Trajectories', *Child Development* 72:1, 187–206.

Bandura, A. and Walters, R.H. (1963), *Social Learning and Personality Development,* (New York: Holt, Reinhart and Winston).

Banks, M., Bates, I., Breakwell, G. and Bynner, J. (1992), *Careers and Identities* (Milton Keynes, Philadelphia: Open University Press).

Barker, R. (1968), *Ecological Psychology* (Stanford, CA: Stanford University Press).

Barnes, C. (1991), *Disabled People in Britain – A Case for Anti-Discrimination Legislation* (London: C. Hurst and Co. Ltd).

Barnes, C. (2002), 'Disability, Policy and Politics', *Policy and Politics* 30, 311–18.

Barnes, C. and Mercer, M. (2005), 'Disability, Work, and Welfare: Challenging the Social Exclusion of Disabled People', *Work, Employment and Society* 19:3, 527–45.

Barnes, C., Mercer, G. and Shakespeare, T. (2003), *Exploring Disability – A Sociological Introduction* (Cambridge: Polity).

Barnes, H., Thornton, P. and Maynard Campbell, S. (1998), *Disabled People and Employment: A Review of Research and Development Work* (Bristol: Policy Press).

Bartley, M. (1994), 'Unemployment and Ill Health: Understanding the Relationships', *Journal of Epidemiology and Community Health* 48, 333–37.

Batcher, W.E. (1982), 'The Influence of the Family on Career selection: A Family Systems Perspective', *The Personnel and Guidance Journal* 61:2, 87–91.

Bates, I. and Riseborough, G. (eds) (1993), *Youth and Inequality* (Buckingham: Open University Press).

BCODP (1986), *Disabled Young People Living Independently* (London: British Council of Organizations of Disabled People).

BCODP (1996), *Directory of Organisations* (Derby: British Council of Disabled People).

Beecher, W. (1998), 'Having a Say! Disabled Children and Effective Partnership', Section 2: Practice Initiatives and Selected Annotated References (London: Council for Disabled Children).

Beresford, B. (1995), *Expert Opinions: A National Survey of Parents Caring for a Severely Disabled Child* (Bristol: Policy Press).

Beresford, B. (1997), *Personal Accounts: Involving Disabled Children in Research* (Norwich: Social Policy Research Unit).

Beresford, B., Sloper P., Baldwin S. and Newman T. (1996), *What Works in Services for Families with a Disabled Child?* (London: Barnardos).

Berthoud, R. (2000), 'Ethnic Employment Penalties in Britain', *Journal of Ethnic and Migration Studies* 26:3, 389–416.

Berthoud, R. (2002), *Multiple Disadvantage in the Labour Market* (York: Joseph Rowntree Foundation).

Berthoud, R. and Blekesaune, M. (2006), *Persistent Employment Disadvantages, 1974 to 2003* (Colchester: University of Essex, Institute for Social Economic Research).

Bignall, T. and Butt, J. (2000), *Between Ambition and Achievement: Young Black Disabled People's Views and Experiences of Independence and Independent Living* (Bristol: The Policy Press Findings, Ref: 340).

Bishop, R. (2001), 'Designing for Special Educational Needs in Mainstream Schools', *Support for Learning* 16:2, 56–63.

Blair, S.L., Blair, M.C.L. and Madamba, A.B. (2003), 'Race/Ethnicity, Gender, and Adolescent's Occupational Aspirations: An Examination of Family Context', *Sociological Studies of Children and Youth* 9, 67–87.

Blau, P.M. and Duncan, O.D. (1967), *The American Occupational Structure* (New York: John Wiley & Sons, Inc).

Boal, A. (2002), *Games for Actors and Non-Actors* (London: Routledge).

Bochner, S. (1994), 'The Effectiveness of Same-sex Versus Opposite-sex Role Models in Advertisements to Reduce Alcohol Consumption in Teenagers', *Addictive Behaviours* 19:1, 69–62.

Bondi, L. (2003), 'Empathy and Identification: Conceptual Resources for Feminist Fieldwork', *ACME: An International E-Journal for Critical Geographies* 2:1, 64–76, URL (consulted July 2004) <http://www.acme-journal.org/vol2/ Bondi. pdf>

Bourdieu, P. (1977a), 'Cultural Reproduction and Social Reproduction', in J. Karabel and A.H. Halsey (eds), *Power and Ideology in Education* (Oxford: Oxford University Press).

Bourdieu, P. (1977b), *Outline of a Theory of Practice* (Cambridge: Cambridge University Press).

Bourdieu, P. and Pearson, J.C. (1990), *Reproduction in Education, Society and Culture* (London: Sage).

British Council of Organizations of Disabled People (1996), *Update no.14 January*.

Brown, D., Brooks, L. and Associates (eds) (1990), *Career Choice and Development, 197–261* (San Francisco: Jossey-Bass).

Brown, S.D. and Lent, R.W. (eds) (2005), *Career Development and Counselling: Putting Theory and Research to Work* (New Jersey: John Wiley and Sons, Inc.).

Brown, M.T. (2004). The Career Development Influence of Family of Origin: Consideration of Race/Ethnic Group Membership and Class. *The Counseling Psychologist* 32:4, 587–95.

Buchanan, A., Daniels, N., Wikler, D., Brock, D.W. and Wilker, D.I. (2000), *From Chance to Choice: Genetics and Justice* (Cambridge: Cambridge University Press).

Burchardt, T. (2000), *Enduring Economic Exclusion: Disabled People, Income and Work* (York: Joseph Rowntree Foundation).

Burchardt, T. (2005), *The Education and Employment of Disabled Young People: Frustrated Ambition* (York: Joseph Rowntree Foundation).

Burgess, E. (2003), *Are We Nearly There Yet: Do Teenage Wheelchair Users Think Integration has been Achieved In Secondary Schools in the UK?* (Whizz-Kidz No Limits Millennium Award).

Bynner, J., Ferri, E. and Shepherd, P. (eds) (1997), *Twenty-something in the 1990s. Getting On, Getting By, Getting Nowhere* (Aldershot: Ashgate).

Cabinet Office (2005), *Improving the Life Chances of Disabled People* (London: Cabinet Office).

Casey, B., Metcalf, H. and Millward, N. (1997), *Employers' Use of Flexible Labour* (London: Policy Studies Institute).

Cassell, C. (1997), 'The Business Case for Equal Opportunities: Implications for Women in Management', *Women in Management Review* 12:1, 11–16.

Centre for Studies in Inclusive Education [website] (2002), (updated 18 May 2006) <http://inclusion.uwe.ac.uk/inclusionweek/index.htm>, accessed 10th July 2006.

Charles, N. and James, E. (2003), 'Gender Work Orientations in Conditions of Job Security', *British Journal of Sociology* 54:2, 239–57.

Chope, R.C. (2006), *Family Matters: The Influence of the Family in Career Decision Making* (Austin: CAPS Press).

Cohen-Scali, V. (2003), 'The Influence of Family, Social, and Work Socialization on the Construction of the Professional Identity of Young Adults', *Journal of Career Development* 29:4, 237–49.

Coldron, J. and Boulton, P. (1991), 'Happiness as a Criterion of Parents' Choice of School', *Journal of Education Policy* 6:2 169–78.

Commission for Racial Equality (1997), *Employment and Unemployment Factsheet* (mdm: CRE).

Conger, R.D., Conger, K.J., Elder, G.H., Lorenz, F.O., Simons, R.L. and Whitbeck, L.B. (1993), 'Family Economic Stress and Adjustment of Early Adolescent Girls', *Developmental Psychology* 29: 206–19.

Cook, T., Swain, J. and French, S. (2001), 'Voices from Segregated Schooling: Towards an Inclusive Education System', *Disability and Society* 16:2, 293–310.

Corbett, J. (2001), *Supporting Inclusive Education: A Connective Pedagogy* (London: Routledge Falmer).

Cullingford, C. (2002), *The Best Years of Their Lives?: Pupils' Experiences of School* (London: Kogan Page Limited).

Davis, J.M. and Watson, N. (2001), 'Where Are the Children's Experiences? Analysing Social and Cultural Exclusion in "Special" and "Mainstream" Schools', *Disability and Society* 16:5, 671–87.

DCSF (2005), *Youth Matters Green Paper* (London: Department for Children Schools and Families).

Department for Education and Employment (2001), *Special Education Needs and Disability Act 2001* (London HMSO).

DfES (2003), *Every Child Matters* (Runcorn: Department for Education and Skills).

Dickens, L. (1994), 'The Business Case for Women's Equality: Is the Carrot Better than the Stick?', *Employee Relations* 16:8, 518.

Dillard, J.M. and Campbell, N.J. (1981), 'Influences of Puerto Rican, Black, and Anglo Parents' Career Behavior on their Adolescent Children's Career Development', *The Vocational Guidance Quarterly* 30: 139–48.

Disability Alliance (1991), *A Way Out of Poverty and Disability: Moving Towards a Comprehensive Disability Income* (London: Disability Alliance).

Disability Rights Commission (2001), *Impact on Small Businesses of Lowering the DDA Part II Threshold* (London: DRC).

Disability Rights Commission (2005), 'Retaining Disabled Employees in Small Businesses: 5 Key Myths – Busted!', *Press Email Bulletin* [10 March] <http://www.drc-gb.org/newsroom/newsdetails.asp?id=791andsection=3>, accessed 10 July 2006

Disability Rights Commission (2006a), 'The Surest Start: Improving the Life Chances of Young Disabled People', *The Disability Debate* <http://www.drc-gb.org/disabilitydebate/priorities/documents/TheSurestStart.pdf>, accessed 30 August 2006.

Disability Rights Commission (2006b), *Welfare Reform Report, January* (London: DRC).

DRC (2003), *Young Disabled People: A Survey of the Views and Experiences of Young Disabled People in Great Britain* (London: Disability Rights Commission).

DRC (2006), *Fitness Standards Investigation* (London: Disability Rights Commission)<http://www.drc-gb.org/Employers_and_Service_Provider/Fitness_Standards_Formal_Inves.aspx>, accessed 7 September 2006.

Dublin, R. (1956), 'Industrial Workers' Worlds: A Study of the Central Life Interest of Industrial Workers', *Social Problems* 3, 131–42.

Duckworth, S. (1995), 'Disability and Equality in Employment – Imperative for a New Approach', Unpublished PhD Thesis (Southampton University, Southampton).

Duffy, S. (2003), *Keys to Citizenship* (Birkenhead: Paradigm).

DWP (2003), *Incapacity Benefit and Severe Disablement Allowance: Quarterly Summary Statistics* <http://www.dwp.gov.uk/asd/asd1/ib_sda_quarterly_-feb03.xls>, accessed 24 March 2006.

Eysenck, H.J. and Cookson, D. (1970), 'Personality in Primary School Children', *British Journal of Educational Psychology* 40, 117–31.

Feldman, M.A. (ed.) (2004), *Early Intervention: The Essential Readings* (Oxford: Blackwell).

Ferry, N.M. (2003), *Turning Points: Adolescents' and Young Adults' Reasoning About Career Choice and Future Employment in Retaining and Attracting Young Adults to the Pennsylvania Heartland* 6-33 retrieved from <http://www.extension.psu.edu/workforce/Briefs/TP_Cover.TOC.pdf> accessed 24 March 2006.

Finch, J. (1984), '"It's Great To Have Someone To Talk To": Ethics and Politics of Interviewing Women', in C. Bell and H. Roberts (eds), *Social Researching: Politics, Problems, Practice*, pp. 70–87 (London: Routledge and Kegan Paul).

Finkelstein, V. (1980), *Attitudes and Disabled People: Issues for Discussion* (New York: World Rehabilitation Fund).

Finkelstein, V. (1993), 'The Commonality of Disability', in J. Swain, V. Finkelstein, S. French and M. Oliver (eds). *Disabling Barriers – Enabling Environments* (London: Sage).

Fischer, M. and Stuber, F. (1998), 'Work Process Knowledge and School-to-Work Transition', in E. Scherer (ed.), *Shop Floor Control: A Systems Perspective* (Berlin: Springer Verlag).

Fisher, T.A. and Griggs, M.B. (1995), 'Factors that Influence the Career Development of African-American and Latino Youth', *The Journal of Vocational Education Research* 20, 57–74.

Fisher, T.A. and Padmawidjaja, I. (1999), 'Parental Influences on Career Development Perceived by African American and Mexican American College Students', *Journal of Multicultural Counseling and Development* 27, 136–52.

Fitzgerald, H., Jobling, A. and Kirk, D. (2003), 'Listening to the "Voices" of Students with Severe Learning Difficulties through a Task-based Approach to Research and Learning in Physical Education', *Support for Learning British Journal of Learning Support* 18:3, 123–9.

Foskett, N., Dyke, M. and Maringe, F. (2003), 'The Influence of the School on the Decision to Participate in Learning Post-16', *Annual Conference of the British Educational Research Association* Edinburgh, Scotland, 11–13 September 2003.

Foskett, N., Dyke, M., and Maringe, F. (2004), 'The Influence of the School in the Decision to Participate in Learning post 16', *DfES Research Report RR538* (Nottingham: DfES).

Foskett, N. and Hemsley-Brown, J. (1999), 'Career Desirability: Young People's Perceptions of Nursing as a Career', *Journal of Advanced Nursing* 29:6, 1342–50.

Foskett, N. and Hemsley-Brown, J. (2001), *Choosing Futures: Young People's Decision-Making in Education, Training and Careers Markets* (London: Routledge Falmer).

Foskett, N.H. and Hesketh, A.J. (1996), *Student Decision-Making in the Post-16 Market Place* (Southampton: HEIST).

French S.A. (1986), 'Handicapped People in Health and Caring Professions: Attitudes, Practices and Experiences', MSc Thesis (South Bank Polytechnic).

Fuchs, D. and Fuchs, L.S. (1998), 'Competing Visions for Educating Students with Disabilities: Inclusion Versus Full Inclusion', *Childhood Education* 74:5, 309–16.

Furlong, A. and Biggart, A. (1999), 'Framing "Choices": A Longitudinal Study of Occupational Aspirations Among 13- to 16-Year-Olds', *Journal of Education and Work* 12:1, 21–35.

Furlong, A. and Cartmel, F. (1995), 'Aspirations and Opportunity Structures: 13-Year-Olds in Areas with Restricted Opportunities', *British Journal of Guidance and Counselling* 23:3, 361–75.

Gerber, P.J., Reiff, H.B. and Ginsberg, R. (1996), 'Reframing the Learning Disabilities Experience', *Journal of Learning Disabilities* 29, 98–101.

Gerson, K. (1993), *No Man's Land: Men's Changing Commitments to Family and Work* (New York: Basic Books).

Gewirtz, S., Ball, S.J. and Bowe, R. (1995), *Markets, Choice and Equity in Education* (Milton Keynes: OUP).

Giddens, A. (1991), *The Constitution of Society: Outline of the Theory of Structuration* (Cambridge: Polity Press).

Giddens, A. (1997), *Sociology*, 3rd Edition (Oxford: Blackwell).

Ginsberg, E., Ginsberg, S.W., Axelrad, S. and Herma, J.L. (1951), *Occupational Choice: An Approach to a General Theory* (New York: Columbia University).

Gottfredson, L.S. (1981), 'Circumscription and Compromise: A Developmental Theory of Occupational Aspirations', *Journal of Counseling Psychology* Monograph 28:6, 545–79.

Gray, P. (2002), *Disability Discrimination in Education: A Review of the Literature of Discrimination Across 0–19 Age Range, Undertaken on Behalf of the Disability Rights Commission* (London: DRC).

Green, A., Leney, T. and Wolf, A. (1999), *Convergence and Divergence in European Education and Training Systems* (London: Bedford Way Papers, Institute of Education, University of London).

Grewal, I., McManus, S., Arthur, S. and Reith, L. (2004), *Making the Transition: Addressing Barriers in Services for Disabled People* (London: Department of Work and Pensions).

Griffin, C. (1985), *Typical Girls? Young Women from School to the Job Market* (London: Routledge).

Grover, C. and Piggott, L. (2005), 'Disabled People, the Reserve Army of Labour and Welfare Reform', *Disability and Society* 20:7, 707–19.

Gruber, J. (2000), 'Disability Employment Benefits and Labor Supply', *Journal of Political Economy* 208:6, 1162–83.

Guichard, J. (1993), *L'école et les représentations d'avenir des adolescents* (Paris: Presses Universitaires de France).

Guile, D. and Griffiths, T. (2001), 'Learning Through Work Experience', *Journal of Education and Work* 14:1, 113–30.

Hall, R.H. (1969), *Occupations and the Social Structure* (London: Prentice-Hall International).

Halsey, A.H., Lauder, H., Brown, P. and Wells, A.S. (1997), *Education: Culture, Economy, and Society* (Oxford: Oxford University Press).

Hansen, J.C. (2005), 'Assessment of Interests', in S.D. Brown and R.W. Lent (eds), *Career Development and Counselling: Putting Theory and Research to Work* (New Jersey: John Wiley and Sons, Inc.).

Hargrove, B.K., Inman, A.G. and Crane, R.L. (2005), 'Family Interaction Patterns, Career Planning Attitudes, and Vocational Identity of High School Adolescents', *Journal of Career Development* 31:4, 263.

Harpaz, I. and Fu, X. (2002). The Structure of the Meaning of Work: A Relative Stability Amidst Change. *Human Relations*, 55, 639–68.

Hart, S. (2008), 'Youth and Citizenship: The Views and Experiences of 1–16-year-olds in Nottingham', Unpublished PhD Thesis (University of Nottingham).

Healy, C. (2003), *A Business Perspective on Workplace Flexibility: When Work Works, An Employer Strategy for the 21st Century* <http://www.familiesandwork.org/3w/research/downloads/cwp.pdf>

Heath, A. and Cheung, S.Y. (2006), *Ethnic Penalties in the Labour Market: Employers and Discrimination* (London: Department for Work and Pensions).

Hendey, N. (1999), *Young Adults and Disability: Transition to Independent Living?* PhD Thesis (University of Nottingham).

Hetherington, E.M. (ed.) (1983), *Socialisation, Personality and Social Development*, *Handbook of Child Psychology 4* (New York: Wiley).

Hill, N.E., Ramirez, C. and Dumka, L.E. (2003), 'Early Adolescents' Career Aspirations: A Qualitative Study of Perceived Barriers and Family Support Among Low-Income, Ethnically Diverse Adolescents', *Journal of Family Issues* 24, 934–59.

Hockey, J. and James, A. (1993), *Growing Up and Growing Older: Ageing and Dependency in the Life Course* (London: Sage).

Hodkinson, P. (2003), 'Learning Careers and Careers Progression', *Learning and Skills Research Journal* 6:3, 24–6.

Hodkinson, P. and Sparkes, A. (1997), 'Careership: a Sociological Theory of Career Decision Making', *British Journal of Sociology of Education* 18:1, 29–44.

Hodkinson, P., Sparkes, A. and Hodkinson, H. (1996), *Triumphs and Tears: Young People, Markets and the Transition from School to Work* (London: David Fulton Publishers).

Hoffman, L.W. (1972), 'Early Childhood Experiences and Women's Achievement Motives', *Journal of Social Issues* 28:2, 129–55.

Holden, C. (1999), 'Globalization, Social Exclusion and Labour's New Work Ethic', *Critical Social Policy* 19:4, 529–38.

Holland, J.L. (1962), 'Some Explorations of a Theory of Vocational Choice: One- and Two-Year Longitudinal Studies,' *Psychological Monographs* 76:26, (Whole No. 545)

Humphries, S. and Gordon, P. (1992), *Out of Sight: The Experience of Disability 1900–1950* (Plymouth: Northcote House Publishers).

Hunter, J.B. (1991), 'Which School? A Study of Parents' Choice of Secondary School', *Educational Research* 33:1, 31–41.

Hussain, Y., Atkin, K. and Ahmad, W. (2002), *South Asian Disabled Young People and their Families* [Social Care, Race and Ethnicity series] (Bristol: The Policy Press).

Jacobsen, M.H. (2000), *Hand-me-down Dreams: How Families Influence our Career Paths* (New York: Three Rivers Press).

James, A. and Prout, A. (1990), 'Contemporary Issues in the Sociological Study Of Childhood', in A. James and A. Prout (eds), *Constructing and Reconstructing Childhood* (London: Falmer Press).

James, A. and Prout, A. (eds) (1990), *Constructing And Reconstructing Childhood* (London: Falmer Press).

Jans, L. (2003), 'Role Models for Youth with Disabilities: Expanding Expectations about Employment and Careers', presented at *Technology and Persons with Disabilities Conference*, California State University.

Jawaan Aur Azaad (1994), *The Road to Freedom* (London: Race Equality Unit).

Jenkinson, J.C. (1997), *Mainstream or Special? Educating Students with Disabilities* (London: Routledge).

Jenkinson, J. (1998), 'Parent Choice in the Education of Students with Disabilities', *International Journal of Disability, Development and Education* 45:2, 189–202.

Joint Committee on the Draft Disability Discrimination Bill (2004), *Draft Disability Discrimination Bill* Vol. 1, Report (London: House of Commons and House of Lords).

Jolly, D. (2000), 'A Critical Evaluation of the Contradictions for Disabled Workers Arising from the Emergence of the Flexible Labour Market in Britain', *Disability and Society* 15:5, 795–810.

Jones, G. and Wallace, C. (1992), *Youth, Family and Citizenship* (Buckingham: Open University Press).

Jussim, L. and Eccles, J. (1992), 'Teacher Expectations II: Construction and Reflection of Student Achievement', *Journal of Personality and Social Psychology* 63, 947–61.

Kagan, C., Lewis, S. and Heaton, P. (1998), *Caring to Work: Accounts of Working Parents of Disabled Children* (London: Family Policy Studies Centre).

Karabel, J. and Halsey, A.H. (eds) (1977), *Power and Ideology in Education* (Oxford: Oxford University Press).

Kenward, H. (ed.) (1996), *Spotlight on Educational Needs* (Tamworth: Nasen).

Kerr, B.A. (1997), *Smart Girls: A New Psychology of Girls, Women, and Giftedness* (Phoenix, AZ: Gifted Psychology).

Kerr, B. (2000), 'Gender and Genius', *Keynote Speech to the National Curriculum Networking Conference*, The College of William and Mary, Arizona State University.

Kerr, B.A. and Erb, C. (1991), Career Counselling with Academically Talented Students: Effects of a Value-Based Intervention', *Journal of Counselling Psychology* 38, 309–14.

Kidd, J.M. (1984), 'Young People's Perceptions of their Occupational Decision Making', *British Journal of Guidance and Counseling* 12:1, 25–38.

Kilsby, M. and Beyer, S. (1996), 'Engagement and Interaction: a Comparison between Supported Employment and ATCs', *Journal of Community and Applied Social Psychology* 6, 141–52.

Labour Force Survey (2001), *Employment Status by Occupation and Sex: Spring 2001* (4 digit SOC) <http://www.statistics.gov.uk/STATBASE/Product. asp?vlnk=14248>, accessed 20 March 2006.

Labour Force Survey (2005), *Employment Status by Occupation and Sex: Spring 2003–2005* (4 digit SOC) <http://www.statistics.gov.uk/STATBASE/Product. asp?vlnk=14248>, accessed 20 March 2006.

Labour Force Survey (2006), *Employment Status by Occupation and Sex: Spring 2004–2006* (4 digit SOC) <http://www.statistics.gov.uk/STATBASE/Product. asp?vlnk=14248>, accessed 20 March 2006.

Leckey, J.F., McGuigan, M.A. and Harrison, R.T. (1995), 'Career Aspirations and Expectations: Does Gender Matter?', *Journal of Further and Higher Education* 19:2, 58–67.

Lee, S., Sills, M. and Gi-Taik, O. (2002), 'Disabilities among Children and Mothers in Low-Income Families, Research in Brief', *US: Institute for Women's Policy Research* <http://www.iwpr.org/pdf/d449.pdf>, accessed 17 October 2006.

Leicester, M. (1999), *Disability Voice – Towards an Enabling Education,. (*London, Philadelphia, PN: Jessica Kingsley Publishers).

Lewis, A. and Lindsay, G. (eds) (2000), *Researching Children's Perspectives* (Buckingham: Open University Press).

Lewis, A., Robertson, C. and Parsons, S. (2005), *Experiences of Disabled Students and their Families*, Phase 1, Research report to Disability Rights Commission, June 2005 (Birmingham: University of Birmingham, School of Education).

Lloyd-Smith, M. and Tarr, J. (2000), 'Researching Children's Perspectives: a Sociological Dimension', in A. Lewis and G. Lindsey (eds), *Researching Children's Perspectives* (Buckingham: Open University Press).

Loumidis, J., Stafford, B., Youngs, R., Green, A., Arthur, S. and Legard, R. (2001), *Evaluation of the New Deal for Disabled People Personal Adviser Service Pilot (No. 144)* (London: DSS).

Lunt, N. and Thornton, P. (1994), 'Disability and Employment: Towards an Understanding of Discourse and Policy', *Disability and Society* 9:2, 223–38.

MacBeath, J., Galton, M., Steward, S., MacBeath, A. and Page, C. (2006), *The Cost of Inclusion* (Cambridge: University of Cambridge Faculty of Education).

Marini, M.M., Fan, P., Finley, E. and Beutel, A.M. (1996), 'Gender and Job Values' *Sociology of Education* 69, 49–65.

Martin, A. (2004), 'Do the Right Thing', *Care and Health Magazine*, September, 24–5.

Martin, J., White, A. and Meltzer, H. (1989), *OPCS Surveys of Disability in Great Britain: Report 4 – Disabled Adults: Services, Transport and Employment* (London: HMSO).

Maton, K., Smyth, K., Broome, S. and Field, P. (2000), *Evaluation of the Effectiveness of Residential Training for Disabled People* (No. 243). Department for Education and Skills.

McDonald, J.L. and Jessell, J.C. (1992), 'Influence of Selected Variables on Occupational Attitudes and Perceived Occupational Abilities of Young Adolescents', *Journal of Career Development* 18, 239–50.

McGinty, J. and Fish, J. (1992), *Learning Support for Young People in Transition* (Milton Keynes: Open University Press).

McHenry, J.J., Hough, L.M., Toquam, J.L., Hanson, M.A. and Ashworth, S. (1990), 'Project A Validity Results: The Relationship Predictor and Criterion domains', *Personnel Psychology* 43, 335–54.

McLoyd, V. C. (1989), 'Socialization and Development in a Changing Economy: The Effects of Paternal Job and Income Loss on Children', *American Psychologist* 44, 293–302.

McLoyd, V. C. (1990), 'The impact of economic hardship on Black families and children: Psychological distress, parenting and socioemotional development', *Child Development* 61, 311–46.

McWhirter, E. H., Hackett, F. and Bandalos, D.L. (1998), 'A Causal Model of the Educational Plans and Career Expectations of Mexican American High School Girls', *Journal of Counseling Psychology* 45,166–81.

Meyer, L. (2001), 'The Impact of Inclusion on Children's Lives: Multiple Outcomes, and Friendship in Particular', *International Journal of Disability, Development and Education* 48, 9–31.

Middleton, L. (1999), *Disabled Children: Challenging Social Exclusion* (Oxford: Blackwell Science Ltd).

Middleton, L. (2003), *Disabled Children: Challenging Social Exclusion* (Oxford: Blackwell Science Ltd).

Mills, C.W. (1959), *The Sociological Imagination* (London: Oxford University Press).

Minuchin, P.P. and Shapiro, P.K. (1983), 'The School as a Context for Social Development', in E.M. Hetherington (ed.) *Socialisation, Personality and Social Development, Handbook of Child Psychology 4* (New York: Wiley).

Morris, J. (1991), *Pride Against Prejudice. Transforming attitudes to disability* (London: The Women's Press Ltd).

Morris, J (1997), 'Care or empowerment? A Disability Rights perspective', *Social Policy and Administration* 31:1, 54–60

Morris, J. (1999), *Supporting Disabled Children and their Families* (Foundations Ref: N79) (York: Joseph Rowntree Foundation)

Morris, J. (2002), *Young Disabled People Moving into Adulthood* (York: JRF Publishing Ltd).

Morrow, V. and Richards, M. (1996a), 'The Ethics of Social Research with Children: An Overview', *Children and Society* 10:2, 90–100.

Morrow, V. and Richards, M. (1996b), *Transitions to Adulthood: A Family Matter?* (York: JRF Publishing Ltd).

Moser, C.A. (1958), *Survey Methods in Social Investigation* (London: Heinemann.)

Neale, B. and Flowerdew, J. (2004), 'Time, Texture and Childhood: The Contours of Longitudinal Qualitative Research', *International Journal of Social Research Methodology* 6:3, 189–201.

Niles, S.G., Herr, E.L. and Hartung, P.J. (2001), 'Achieving Life Balance: Myths, Realities, and Developmental Perspectives', *Information Series No. 387, Ohio State University* <http://www-tcall.tamu.edu/erica/docs/niles/niles1.pdf>, accessed 17 January 2006.

NOP (2003), *A Survey of the Views and Experiences of Young Disabled People in Great Britain*, conducted by NOP on behalf of the Disability Rights Commission (London: DRC).

Norwich, B. (1997), Exploring the Perspectives of Adults with Moderate Learning Difficulties on their Special Schooling and Themselves: Stigma and Self-Perceptions; *European Journal of Special Education* 12:1, 38–53.

Oakley, A. (1981), 'Interviewing Women: A Contradiction in Terms', in H. Roberts (ed.) *Doing Feminist Research* (London: Routledge).

Ofsted, (2004), *Special Educational Needs and Disability: Towards Inclusive Schools* (London: Audit Commission).

Ofsted, (2006), *Inclusion: Does it Matter Where Pupils Are Taught?* <http://www.ofsted.gov.uk/publications/2535>

Office for National Statistics (2003), *Economic Activity of Working Aged People with Disabilities* <http://www.statstics.gov.uk/downloads/theme_labour/lfsqs_0803.pdf>, accessed 20 March 2006.

O'Kane, C. (2000), 'The Development of Participatory Techniques: Facilitating Children's Views about Decisions which Affect Them', in P. Christensen and A. James (eds), *Research with Children Perspectives and Practices* (London: Falmer Press).

Otto, L.B. (2000), 'Youth Perspectives on Parental Career Influence', *Journal of Career Development* 27:2, 111–19.

Ouchman, J. (1996), 'The Effects of Nongender-role Stereotyped, Same-sex Role Models in Storybooks on the Self-esteem of Children in Grade Three', *Sex Roles* 35, 711–33.

Palmer, G., Carr, J. and Kenway, P. (2005), *Monitoring Poverty and Social Exclusion* (York: Joseph Rowntree Foundation).

Palmer, G., McInnes, T. and Kenway, P. (2006), *Monitoring Poverty and Social Exclusion* (York: Joseph Rowntree Foundation).

Parish, S.L and Cloud, J.M. (2006), 'Child Care for Low-income School-age Children: Disability and Family Structure Effects in a National Sample', *Children and Youth Services Review* 28, 927–40.

Pascall, G. and Hendey, N. (2004), 'Disability and Transition to Adulthood: the Politics of Parenting', *Critical Social Policy* 24:2, 165–86.

Pattie, C., Seyd, P. and Whiteley, P. (2004), *Citizenship in Britain: Values, Participation and Democracy* (Cambridge: Cambridge University Press).

Philpott, S. and Sait, W. (2001), 'Disabled Children: An Emergency Submerged', in Priestley (ed.) *Disability and the Life Course: Global Perspectives* (Cambridge: Cambridge University Press).

Pitt, V. and Curtin, M. (2004), 'Integration Versus Segregation: the Experiences of a Group of Disabled Students Moving from Mainstream School into Special Needs Further Education', *Disability and Society* 19:4, 387–400.

Powney, J. and Lowden, K. (2000), 'Young People's Life-skills and Work', *The Scottish Council for Research in Education* (Edinburgh: SCRE).

Priestley, M. (1997), 'The Origins of a Legislative Disability Category in England: a Speculative History', *Disability Studies Quarterly* 17:2, 87–94.

Priestley, M. (1998), 'Childhood Disability and Disabled Childhoods' *Childhood – A Global Journal of Child Research* 5:2, 207–23.

Priestley, M. (1999), 'Discourse and Identity: disabled children in mainstream High Schools', in S. French and M. Corker (eds), *Disability Discourse*, (Buckingham: Open University Press) pp. 92–102.

Priestley, M. (ed.) (2001), *Disability and the Life Course: Global Perspectives* (Cambridge: Cambridge University Press).

Priestley, M. (2003), *Disability. A Life Course Approach* (Cambridge: Polity Press in association with Blackwell Publishing Company).

Prout, A. (2001), 'Representing Children: Reflections on the Children 5–16 Programme', *Children and Society* 15, 193–201.

Putnam, J.W. (1993), *Cooperative Learning and Strategies for Inclusion: Celebrating Diversity in the Classroom* (Baltimore: MD Brookes).

Read, J. and Clements, L. (2001), *Disabled Children and the Law: Research and Good Practice* (London: Jessica Kingsley Publishers).

Reay, D. (1996), 'Insider Perspectives of Stealing the Words Out of Women's Mouths: Interpretation in the Research Process', *Feminist Review* 53, 57–73.

Reay, D. and Ball, S.J. (1998), 'Making Their Minds Up': Family Dynamics of School Choice', *British Educational Research Journal* 24:4, 431–48.

Reiser, R. (1995), 'Developing a Whole-School Approach to Inclusion: Making the Most of the Code and 1993 Act: A Personal View', *Discussion Paper III. Schools' Special Needs Policies Pack* (London: National Children's Bureau).

Riddell, S., Baron, S. and Wilson, A. (2001), 'The Significance of the Learning Society for Women and Men with Learning Difficulties', *Gender and Education* 13:1, 57–73.

Roberson, L. A. and Parsons, S. (2005), *DRC Research Report – Experiences of Disabled Students and their Families: Phase 1* (London: DRC).

Roberts, C.M. and Smith, P. R. (1999), 'Attitudes and Behaviour of Children towards Peers with Disabilities', *International Journal of Disability, Development and Education* 46:1, 35–49.

Roberts, K. (1995), *Youth Employment in Modern Britain* (Oxford: Oxford University Press).

Robinson, C. and Stalker, K. (1998), 'Introduction' in C. Robinson and K. Stalker (eds). *Growing Up With Disability* (London: Jessica Kingsley Publications).

Robinson, C. and Stalker, K. (eds) (1998), *Growing Up With Disability* (London: Jessica Kingsley Publications).

Roe, A. (1956), *Psychology of Occupations* (New York: Wiley).

Rose, A.M. (ed.) (1962), *Human Behaviour and Social Processes: An Interactionist Approach* (London: Routledge and Kegan Paul).

Russell, F. (2003), 'The Expectations of Parents of Disabled Children', *British Journal of Special Education* 20:3, 144–9.

Russell, P. (1998) *Having a Say: Disabled Children and Effective Partnership in Decision Making, Section 1: The Report* (London: Council For Disabled Children).

Russell Commission (2005), *The Russell Commission on Youth Action and Engagement: Consultation* (Norwich: HMSO).

Scherer, E. (ed.) (1998), *Shop Floor Control: A Systems Perspective* (Berlin: Springer Verlag).

Schulenberg, J.E., Vondracek, F.W. and Crouter, A.C. (1984), 'The Influence of the Family on Vocational Development', *Journal of Marriage and the Family* 46, 129–141.

Shah, S. (2005a), *Career Success of Disabled High-Flyers* (London: Jessica Kingsley Publishers).

Shah, S. (2005b), 'Choices and Voices: The Educational Experiences of Young Disabled People, Career Research and Development', *The NICEC Journal* 12, 20–26.

Shah, S. (2006), 'Sharing the Same World: The Researcher and the Researched', *Qualitative Research* 6:2, 207–20.

Shah, S. (2007), 'Special or Mainstream? – The Views of Disabled Students', *Research Papers in Education* (London: Routledge).

Shah, S., Travers, C. and Arnold, J. (2004a), 'Disabled and Successful: Education in the Life Stories of Disabled High Achievers', *Journal of Research in Special Educational Needs* 4:3, 122–32.

Shah, S., Travers, C., and Arnold, J. (2004b), 'The Impact of Childhood on Disabled Professionals', *Children and Society* 18, 194–206.

Shakespeare T. and Watson N. (1998), 'Social Class, Parental Encouragement and Educational Aspirations', *American Journal of Sociology* 73, 559–72.

Shaw, L. (1998), 'Children's Experiences of School' in C. Robinson and K. Stalker (eds), *Growing Up With Disability* (London: Jessica Kingsley Publications).

Sloper, T. and Beresford, B. (2006), 'Families with Disabled Children', *British Medical Journal* 333, 928–9.

Small, J. and McClean, M. (2002), 'Factors Impacting on the Choice of Entrepreneurship as a Career by Barbadian Youth: A Preliminary Assessment', *Journal of Eastern Carribean Studies* 27:4, 30–54.

Smith, A. and Twomey, B. (2002), 'Labour Market Experiences of People with Disabilities' *Labour Market Trends*, August, 415–27.

Stanley, L. and Wise, S. (1993), *Breaking Out Again: Feminist Ontology and Epistemology* (London: Routledge).

Steinberg, L. (2002), *Adolescence* (New York: McGraw-Hill).

Stone, D. (1984), *The Disabled State* (Philadelphia: Temple University Press).

Strategy Unit (2003), *Ethnic Minorities and the Labour Market. Final Report* (London: Cabinet Office).

Strauss, A. (1962), 'Transformations of Identity', in Rose (ed.), *Human Behaviour and Social Processes: An Interactionist Approach* (London: Routledge and Kegan Paul).

Strong, E.K. (1943), *Vocational Interests of Men and Women* (Palo Alto, CA: Stanford University Press).

Such, E., Walker, O. and Walker, R. (2005), 'Anti-War Children: Representation of Youth Protests against the Second Iraq War in the British National Press', *Childhood* 12:3, 301–26.

Super, D.E. (1990), 'A Life-span, Life-space Approach to Career Development', in D. Brown, L. Brooks and Associates (eds), *Career Choice and Development, 197–261* (San Francisco: Jossey-Bass).

Sutherland, A. (1981), *Disabled We Stand* (London: Souvenir Press).

Swain, J., French, S., Barnes, C. and Thomas, C. (eds) (2004), *Disabling Barriers Enabling Environments* (London: Sage/Open University Press).

Swanson, J.L. and Woike, M.B. (1997), 'Theory into Practice in Career Assessment for Women: Assessment and Interventions Regarding Perceived Career Barriers', *Journal of Career Assessment* 5, 431–50.

Tajfel, H. and Fraser, C. (1978), *Introducing Social Psychology* (Harmondsworth: Penguin).

Tannock, S. and Flocks, S. (2003), '"I Know What It's Like to Struggle": The Working Lives of Young Students in an Urban Community College', *Labor Studies Journal* 28:1, Spring, 1–30.

Taylor, B.J., McGilloway, S. and Donnelly, M. (2004), 'Preparing Young Adults with Disability for Employment', *Health and Social Care in the Community* 12:2, 93–101.

Taylor, G. and Palfreman-Kay J.M. (2000), 'Helping Each Other: Relations Between Disabled and Non-disabled Students on Access Programmes', *Journal of Further and Higher Education* 24:1, 39–53.

Thomas, C. (1998), 'Parents and Family: Disabled Women's Stories About their Childhood Experiences' in C. Robinson and K. Stalker (eds), *Growing Up With Disability* (London: Jessica Kingsley Publications).

Tomlinson, S. (1982), *The Sociology of Special Education* (London: Routledge and Kegan Paul).

Tomlinson, S. (ed.) (1994), *Educational Reform and its Consequences* (London: Institute for Public Policy Research and Rivers Oram Press).

Tomlinson, S. and Colquhoun, R. (1995), 'The Political Economy of Special Educational Needs in Britain', *Disability and Society* 10:2, 191–202.

Trankina, M. (1992), 'Racio-ethnic Differences in Confidence in Science', *Psychological Reports* 71, 235–42.

Trice, A.D., Hughes, A.M., Odom, C., Woods, K. and McClellan, N.C. (1995), 'The Origins of Children's Career Aspirations IV: Testing Hypotheses from Four Theories', *The Career Development Quarterly* 43:307–32.

Tuckett, A. (1997), *Life Long Learning in England and Wales: An Overview and Guide to Issues Arising from the European Year of Lifelong Learning* (Leicester: National Organization for Adult Learning).

Union of Physically Impaired Against Segregation/Disability Alliance (1976), *Fundamental Principles of Disability* (London: UPIAS/Disability Alliance).

Vernon, A. (1997), 'Reflexivity: The Dilemmas of Researching from the Inside', in C. Barnes and G. Mercer (eds) *Doing Disability Research* (Leeds: The Disability Press).

Vickerstaff, S. (2003), 'Education and Training', in J. Baldock, N. Manning and S. Vickerstaff (eds), *Social Policy* (Oxford: Oxford University Press).

Vlachou, A.D. (1997), *Struggles for Inclusive Education* (Buckingham: Open University Press).

Vondracek, F.W., Lerner, R.M. and Schulenberg, J.M. (1986), *Career Development: A Life Span Approach* (Hillsdale, NJ: Lawrence Erlbaum).

Vroom, V.H. (1964); *Work and Motivation* (London: John Wiley & Sons).

Walker, A. (1982), *Unqualified and Underemployed* (Basingstoke: Macmillan/National Children's Bureau).

Warnock, M. (2005), 'Special Educational Needs: A New Look', *Journal of Philosophy of Education*, No. 11 in a series of policy discussions.

Warr, P. (1985), 'Twelve Questions About Unemployment and Health', in B. Roberts, R. Finnegan and G. Gallie (eds), *New Approaches to Economic Life* (Manchester: Manchester University Press).

Watson, N., Shakespeare, T., Cunningham-Burley, S., Barnes, C., Corker, M., Davis, J. and Priestly, M. (1999), *Life as a Disabled Child: A Qualitative Study of Young People's Experiences and Perspectives: Final Report* (Edinburgh and Leeds: Universities of Edinburgh and Leeds).

Wertheimer, A. (1997), *Inclusive Education: A Framework for Change; National and International Perspectives* (Leicester: Centre for Studies on Inclusive Education).

Werts, C.E. and Watley D.J. (1972), 'Parental influence on Talent Development' *Journal of Counseling Psychology* 19, 367–72.

West, A. and Varlaam, A. (1991a), 'Choice of High Schools: Pupils' Perceptions', *Educational Research* 33:3, 205–15.

West, A. and Varlaam, A. (1991b), 'Choosing a Secondary School: Parents of Junior School Children', *Educational Research* 33:1, 22–9.

Whiston, S.C. and Keller, B.K. (2004), 'The Influences of the Family of Origin on Career Development: A Review and Analysis', *The Counseling Psychologist,* 32:4, 493–568.

White, B., Cox, C., and Cooper, C. (1992), *Women's Career Development: A Study of High Flyers* (Oxford: Blackwell Publishers)

Woelfel, J. and Haller, A.O. (1971), 'Significant Others, the Self-Reflexive Act and the Attitude Formation Process', *American Sociological Review* 36:1 74–87.

Wohlford, K.E., Lochman, J.E. and Barry, T.D. (2004), 'The Relation Between Chosen Role Models and the Self-Esteem of Men and Women', *Sex Roles* 50: 7–8, 575–82(8).

Wolbring, G. (2001), 'Where Do We Draw the Line? Surviving Eugenics in a Technological World', in M. Priestley (ed.), *Disability and the Life Course: Global Perspectives* (Cambridge: Cambridge University Press).

Wood, M. (1973), *Children: The Development of Personality and Behaviour* (London: Harrap).

Woodland, S., Simmonds, N., Thornby, M., Fitzgerald, R. and McGee, A. (2003), *The Second Work Life Balance Study: Results from the Employer's Survey – Executive Summary* (London: National Centre for Social Research, Department of Trade and Industry).

Wright, S. (2005), 'Young People's Decision-Making in 14–19 education and Training: A Review of the Literature', *The Nuffield Review of Years 14–19 Education and Training* (Oxford: University of Oxford).

Young, G. (1981) 'A Woman in Medicine: Reflections from the Inside', in H. Roberts (ed.), *Women, Health and Reproduction* (London: Routledge & Kegan Paul).

Index

ability, and social class 79
  see also disability
Abrams, F., *Inclusion is Just an
    Illusion* 51
Access to Work (AtW) programme 3,
    18–19, 26, 66
  work experience, non-applicability
    to 26, 62, 97
Aynsley-Green, Al 3–4

Bandura, A., social learning theory 32
benefit claimants, disabled people 17
benefit exit, and PAS 18
Bourdieu, Pierre 15, 32, 38
  habitus concept 23
British Council of Disabled People
    (BCODP) 19, 58

Cabinet Office, *Improving the
    Life Chances of Disabled
    People* 17–18, 93, 99
career choices 20–1
  and education 49
  family influence 80
  institutions, role 22–3
  life cycle factors 21
  and role models 88
  and SCCT 32, 37–8
  social/individual determinants 38–9
  transitions 22
  turning points 21–2
  young disabled people 38–47,
    97–8
Carer's Grant 99
Centre for Studies on Inclusive
    Education (CSIE) 75

Children's Commissioner 3–4
class *see* social class
Contact a Family organization 100

decision making, young people 40
development theory, Ginzberg 32
Direct Payment Scheme 99
disability
  changing views of 20
  medical model stereotype 36, 63,
    77, 79, 84, 88, 98
  social construction of 44–5
Disability Discrimination Act (DDA)
    (1995/2005) 3, 5, 26, 50, 52,
    93
  work experience, non-
    applicability 26, 62, 66, 97
Disability Equality Duty (2006) 50
Disability Rights Commission 3
Disability Task Force 3
Disabled Facilities Grant 99
disabled people
  benefit claimants 17
  early retirement 2
  earnings 2, 100
  employment
    rates 29
    targets 2
  life chances 45
  recruitment level 28
  underemployment 2
  unemployment 2
  working conditions, adverse 19
  workplace adjustments 29
  see also young disabled people
doctors, image of 1

earnings, disabled people 2, 100
education
    and career choices 49
    and the workforce 49–50
employment
    and ethnicity 41–2
    and gender 42–3
    and status 1, 15–16
    see also work
Equality 2025: 93
ethnicity, and employment 41–2
*Every Child Matters: Change for
    Children* 99
Every Child Matters programme 91

family
    career choices, influence on 80
    and identity construction 78
    influence 78, 79–81, 98
    role 77–8
        models 88–91, 92
    and social class 78–9, 83, 99
    young disabled people
        non-supportive 84–7
        supportive 81–4
flexible working 16–17
    disadvantages 20

gender
    and employment 42–3
        young disabled people 43–4
    and identity 97–8
Ginzberg, E., development theory 32

habitus concept
    Bourdieu 23
    example 23–4
high-flyers, disabled 16, 28
human right, work as 19
Human Rights Act (1998) 5

Identification and Assessment of
    Special Educational Needs,
    Code of Practice 5
identity

construction, and the family 78
    and gender 97–8
Incapacity Bill 93
Individual Budgets programme 99
individuals, and society 93
Innovative Schemes 18

Jobcentre Plus 2

Labour Force Survey (2006) 17

Macbeath, J., *The Cost of Inclusion* 51
'Meaning of Work' (MOW) project 16
medical model stereotype,
    disability 36, 63, 77, 79, 84,
    88, 98
mental health, work, connection 16
mental illness, unemployment,
    connection 16

National Council for Work
    Experience 60
National Framework for Organizations
    of Disabled People
    (NFODP) 18
National Service Framework 91
New Deal for Disabled People
    (NDDP) 2, 18, 28, 93
    participation 19
New Deal for Young People 3
nursing, young people's perception of
    42–3

occupational choices, young disabled
    people 32–3
Office for Disability Issues (ODI),
    establishment 18

Palmer, G., *Monitoring Poverty and
    Social Exclusion* 100
Pathways to Work initiative 3, 18, 93
    participation 19
    pilot schemes 19

person-centred planning, young
    disabled people 27
Personal Advisor Service (PAS) 2
    and benefit exit 18
Pupil Referral Units 9, 57, 70, 96

Residential Training Scheme 29
role models
    and career choices 88
    family as 88–91, 92
    parent's profession 90–1
    same-sex 89–90
Russell Commission report 64, 66

school-to-work, transition 24–9
schools
    friendships/social
        relationships 70–4
    mainstream 50–1, 55, 58, 67, 68,
        71, 75, 95, 96
    negative experiences 54, 67, 68, 95
    positive experiences 53–4, 66–8, 95
    post-school choices 53–60
    special 24, 46, 56–9, 66–7, 70,
        71–2, 95, 96
    teachers' expectations 54
    teaching assistants 68–70
    see also work experience
Shah, S., *Career Success of Disabled
    High-Flyers* 16
social class
    and ability 79
    and family 78–9, 83, 99
social cognitive career theory (SCCT),
    and career choices 32, 37–8
social exclusion, and work 19
social learning theory, Bandura 32
society, and individuals 93
special education, disadvantages 63–4,
    74–5
    see also schools, special
Special Educational Needs
    Coordinators (SENCOs) 11,
    37, 55, 65

Special Educational Needs and
    Disability Act (2001) 5, 50, 52
status, and employment 1, 15–16

teaching assistants 68–70
    disadvantages 68–9, 75, 96
    misuse of 70
Training Credit scheme 43
transitions
    career choices 22
    school-to-work 24–9

unemployment
    disabled people 2
    mental illness, connection 16
    young disabled people 17

Vocational Opportunities in Training
    for Employment (VOTE) 29

Warnock, Baroness Mary 51, 67
Welfare Reform Bill 93
welfare reform initiatives 18–19
'welfare to work' strategies 18
work
    as human right 19
    mental health, connection 16
    and social exclusion 19
    see also employment; work
        experience
work experience 60–6
    AtW, non-applicability 26, 62, 97
    benefits 60–1
    and career aspirations 61–2, 64, 75
    DDA, non-applicability 26, 62,
        66, 97
    limitations 62–3, 66
    obstacles 62, 64–5, 75
    and risk-averse culture 62, 75
    school/workplace partnerships 65–6
Work and Pensions, Dept, schemes 3
work-life balance 16
workforce, and education 49–50

working conditions, adverse, and
disabled people 19
workplace culture, changing 19

young disabled people 1
    aspirations 2, 4, 12–13, 46–7
    career choices 38–47, 97
        gender influences 43–4
        gender-typical 97–8
    change, views on 100–2
    costs of bringing up 85
    definition 6
    dependency 5
        on parents 26
    educational opportunities 50,
        52–3, 95, 96
        family influences 80–1
        see also schools
    families
        as role models 88–91, 92
        supportive 81–4
        unsupportive 84–7
    goals 32–4

    compromised 35–6
    realistic 34–5
    integration 26, 51, 57, 96
    lone-parent families 85
    occupational choices 32–3
    over protection 27, 81
    person-centred planning 27
    support
        needs 100
        non-family 87
    unemployment 17
    views, seeking 4–5, 6, 94
young disabled people study
    classroom observation 12
    data collection 11–13
    education, experience of 13
    family influences 13, 46
    forum theatre workshops 12
    interviews 12
    participants 7–9
    qualitative approach 10
    researcher bias 10–11
young people, decision making 40